BURY A CENTURY AGO

£3.60

This book is a reprint of part of a book first published in 1889
by The Historical Publishing Company.

The introductory essay is by Frank Sunderland.

Landy Publishing
3 Staining Rise
Staining, Blackpool FY3 0BU
Tel: (0253) 886103

ISBN: 0 9507692 9 0

Printed by Galava Printing Company Limited, Nelson, Lancashire

BURY A CENTURY AGO

with Introduction by
Frank Sunderland

Landy Publishing
1990

Preface

The main part of this book is reproduced from one first published in 1889 - a century ago. Its title extended to seven lines, and it was intended as the first part of a series of books showing the cities and towns of Lancashire, *"the premier county of the kingdom"*, giving details of the towns' history, their statistics and telling of their businesses. This latter aspect amounted to giving potted histories of the firms listed. Of course, they had paid for the advert (for that's what it was) and those which hadn't paid didn't get a mention.

The book's preface declared its object as *"portraying with all possible clearness the prominent phases of Lancashire's commercial greatness"* and went on to say that the book would *"better acquaint the businessman with his fellows in commerce, and more fully familiarise the buyer with the seller."* It is most likely that most businesses were represented in its pages and would have some say in what was written about their company, giving today's reader a window to look through at a commercial era that has passed into history. Just as today's directories have companies making electronic equipment, so did yesterday's companies make such items as healds and reeds to support the cotton sheds. Then as now, the companies of a town were inter-related and inter-dependent .... In short, this part of the book is a *"Yellow Pages"* - with body.

To pump life into the list of businesses, local historian Frank Sunderland has written an essay which will introduce the reader to the Bury of a century ago, when the looms whirred and the dark Satanic mills belched forth their muck - which made wages and profits that could be spent with the town's shopkeepers and tradesmen. Frank has also provided some photographs from his extensive collection.

Also reproduced is material from local directories which gives an insight into what was happening in Bury a century ago, and which companies were advertising their quality.

The publisher is grateful to Frank Sunderland and Mrs Rita Hirst of Bury Library for their help in finding material, to Gerry and Kevin Burke for use of their photographs and to others who have helped in bringing this book to the notice of Bury folk, descendants of those who worked in the firms listed - just five generations back.

Please step back in time and enjoy the Bury of a century ago.

Landy Publishing

Introduction

A century ago, in 1889, the Historical Publishing Company published as the first of a projected series of books on Lancashire, a volume covering Bolton, Bury, Ramsbottom, Lancaster, Ulverston, Barrow, Preston, Chorley, Blackburn, Darwen, Southport, Ormskirk, Blackpool and Fleetwood.

It was written and produced in a style very typical of the later years of Victoria's long reign, when Britain enjoyed an unrivalled period of peace, prosperity, and advancement. True enough, we usually had a small colonial war going in distant places, but not amounting to any great disturbance of life in Britain. The despatch of a gunboat or two with a small detachment of soldiery was usually enough to put the "*natives*" in their place and add another patch of red to our world atlas of Empire.

These settled years saw a Britain increasingly better housed and fed, with increasingly higher standards of health and hygiene, education, and prosperity generally, with a strong claim to world supremacy.

The Lancashire textile industry was easily Britain's - and the world's - greatest, and here in the North West it had spawned all kinds of ancillary industries, some of which, such as engineering, chemicals, and paper, were emerging as giants in their own right. Bury was close to the centre of all this, and proof of the town's importance was the grant of a charter of incorporation as a County Borough in 1876.

The Historical Publishing Company appears to have been a somewhat entrepreneurial outfit, which, alas, failed to attain the pinnacles of fame and prosperity, and the omissions in their list of canvassed local manufacturers and trades is somewhat disappointing. Nevertheless, at this distance in time, and with our awakened interest in times past, they can be seen to have performed a signal service for posterity, and those few firms listed then which survive to the present day will no doubt be gratified, and maybe surprised, to read of their earlier days.

A Rip Van Winkle awakening from his century-old sleep to re-visit his home town of Bury to-day would need a great deal of adjustment to bring into focus the Bury of 1989.

To begin with, he would find the name "*Bury*" must now be qualified to distinguish between the old County Borough and the triple-sized "*Metropolitan Borough*" which now includes Prestwich, Radcliffe, Ramsbottom, Tottington, and Whitefield. But even the old County Borough has expanded outwards, taking in green fields on almost all sides to make way for vastly improved housing, roads, schools and the like. He would, one hopes, mark with approval the increased greenery by way of gardens, trees, and open spaces generally.

Although at weekends he might feel re-assured (only since 1987 and by virtue of volunteer amateurs) by the sight of a steam train wending its way on the old East Lancashire/Lancashire and Yorkshire line up the Irwell valley towards Ramsbottom, this would hardly compensate for his dismay in finding the newly opened (in 1879) line from Manchester via Prestwich, Whitefield, and Radcliffe to be the last surviving link with the national rail network, and that no longer could he visit Holcombe Tower by way of the Holcombe Branch Line (opened 1882, closed 1960), or to Rawtenstall (opened 1848, closed 1972), or travel to Accrington (opened 1848, closed 1960). And sadly, he would find that popular line from Knowsley Street Station to Bolton, Preston, and the Fylde Coast or (in the easterly direction), to Rochdale, Leeds, York, and the east coast, catering, in 1889, to the fast growing numbers of factory folk desirous of tasting the sea air, was closed in 1970 after 122 years.

Our newly awakened friend might be tempted to take another sleeping draught after seeing our roads all busy with horseless carriages - entirely absent in his day -now travelling at hair-raising speeds which would seem incredible after the steady plodding of horses, and especially so if he was at Bury Bridge during rush hours! Maybe (unless he was a keen gardener!) he would find some compensation in the absence of the thousands of tons of horse manure formerly deposited annually on Bury's streets.

Even in 1889 the Bury Bridge wharf, terminus of the Manchester-Bolton-Bury Canal, would have seemed an outmoded place, although still well used and carrying a good annual tonnage, mainly of coal, but also including raw cotton, timber, stone, etc. But a century later all trace has disappeared and he would have to trudge a good half mile almost to Elton Reservoir to reach the stagnant, disused new terminus of the canal, now in water only to Little Lever. His bemusement would no doubt change to utter bewilderment to learn that in 1989 this truncated canal was under consideration as part of a wider plan **to attract tourists to Bury**!

In 1889, unlike many Lancashire towns, Bury's textile industry was far from being confined to cotton fibres. In fact the town had a thriving woollen textile trade which still survives, specialising mainly in industrial felts. The whole textile industry is but a shadow of its former self, cotton has been almost entirely displaced by artificial fibres, but the dyeing, bleaching, and finishing of textiles is still around.

The Irwell valley between Ramsbottom and Ringley has seen 25 paper mills in production, which made it the heaviest concentration of paper manufacture in Britain, accounting for nearly 10% of the national output. Although many of these mills have disappeared, new machinery and modern technology have made for increased output with far fewer sites - and workers. Bury itself has a large chunk of this paper-making, and, until recently, could lay claim to be one of the world's biggest centres of the manufacture of paper-making machinery. The earliest Bury paper mill was at Bridge Hall as early as 1716 (because all new paper had to be taken to Stationer's Hall in London to pay duty and be stamped, early paper-making in England tended to be confined to the south-east, until this tax was repealed). In Lancashire the greatest name in paper was Crompton, and one of several branches of that family, J.R. Crompton, began paper-making at the Elton mill in 1853. That same mill, described in such detail in 1889, is still in production, with other, later, branches still operating at Simpson Clough and at Lydney in Gloucestershire.

In the country as a whole, manufacturing industries have greatly declined in the last decade or two. This is especially true for the North West, and Bury has shared in this regrettable trend. Even forty years ago it was easy to count well over one hundred tall mill chimneys from the high ground overlooking Bury, but to-day barely a score survive, although the drift away from coal-fired steam power has accounted for part of the decline. On the credit side one must welcome the marked decrease in atmospheric pollution which has meant appreciable increases in hours of sunshine annually, and has given gardeners a wider choice of trees, shrubs, and plants which could not formerly have been reared in the polluted air. Ironically, "*black spot*" on roses, and other now common fungus spots on trees such as sycamore, are present to-day but could not have survived in the pollution of past years.

The final blow to horse-drawn passenger transport in Bury was the appearance of steam trams on 12th March, 1883, under the Manchester, Bury, Rochdale, and Oldham Steam Tramways Company, Ltd., using a track from Blackford Bridge to the Market Place. Routes to Limefield, Tottington, and Heap Bridge quickly followed. At that time the route outwards by way of Fleet Street, Rock Street, Stanley Street, and Water Street (since 1935 all combined as "*The Rock*") was narrow and confined, and due to opposition from the Rector of Bury steam trams were forbidden to use it, having to reach the tram depot at the Castle Armoury in The Wylde by way of Market Street, Princess Street, and Rochdale Road. This veto was withdrawn when Rock Street was widened in 1886.

The days of steam power for tram traction were already numbered when the service began in 1883, for at a meeting that same year in Bury of the Association of Municipal Engineers, the Engineer of the Tramway Company, Mr. Vauser, declared "*There is every reason to believe that tramways at no distant date will be propelled by electricity*". The self-same week that steam trams began in Bury trials of electric traction methods were being held in London, from Uxbridge Road to Kew Bridge.

Fumes, grit and smoke, not to mention a bumpy ride by the steam traction unit, (a separate vehicle towing the passenger car) were a source of annoyance and complaint, but it was 3rd June, 1903 before electric trams, now Corporation owned, began a service from Moorside to Jericho, to be quickly followed by a network serving Bury and neighbouring towns with connections all over South East Lancashire. These ran at very frequent invervals, e.g. in the 1920s the Manchester to Whitefield service was every six minutes and the fare was fourpence (4d).

Not everywhere was served by trams, and the Bury Walshaw was one such route, but Bury's first omnibus service remedied this deficiency, commencing on 19th September, 1925. A service to Ainsworth began in the next year, and from that time onwards trams steadily gave way to motor buses, although the Second World War delayed the process and the very last tram ran on the 13th February, 1949, on the Walmersley route.

When Bury Corporation took over the tramways a new depot was needed, and on 23rd July, 1902, the foundation stone was laid for the premises in Rochdale Road, which were replaced and demolished in 1987. By this time the Transport Department was no longer Bury owned, having passed in 1969 to SELNEC (*South East Lancashire and North East Cheshire*) Transport system, serving the whole of the Manchester conurbation. When Greater Manchester County was created in 1974, this became G.M. Transport, who still administer the regional service, now under the name of Passenger Transport Executive.

The Bury Loyal Association of Volunteers has long since gone, even before 1889, but a proud local military tradition has been continued, this by the famous infantry regiment whose origins date back to 1688, being known successively as *"Peyton's Own"*, *"The XX or East Devon Regiment of Foot"*, and then from 1st July, 1881 as *"XX The Lancashire Fusiliers"*. The depot remained at Exeter until 1873, but when the regiment became The Lancashire Fusiliers they occupied the newly built Wellington Barracks in Elton. In 1968 the Regiment was absorbed into *"The Royal Regiment of Fusiliers"*. The battle honours were almost innumerable. During the 1914-18 War 30 battalions were formed, and collected 18 Victoria Crosses, this being more than any other regiment in the British Army, and including the famous *"Six before breakfast"* at the bloody Gallipoli landings in April, 1915.

Almost all of the Wellington Barracks were demolished in the late 1960s, leaving little more than the Regimental Museum, although the Castle Armoury and Drill Hall on the site of the former Bury Castle in the town centre still serves the Territorial Army.

The Bury Banking Company's handsome building of 1867 still stands in Silver Street, but in 1888 the Company amalgamated with the Lancashire and Yorkshire Bank, who in 1928 became Martin's Bank, which in turn was absorbed by Barclay's Bank, the present occupants.

That fine facade comprising the Derby Hotel, Derby Hall, and Atheneum, commissioned by the Earl of Derby in 1850, with Sir Sidney Smirke as architect, was an asset to any town, but, sadly, in 1965 the Derby Hotel was demolished, and later the Atheneum, leaving only the Derby Hall, now the home of Bury Metro Arts Association. The Atheneum Club still survives, now in the former Education Department offices in Moss Street.

BURY.

RESOURCES, INDUSTRIES, AND GROWTH.

THE busy manufacturing town of Bury, which one hundred years ago did not contain three thousand inhabitants, but which has now twenty times that number, is a typical Lancashire community, connected at once with the traditions of the past and the busy practical business of the present. It was held by the De Lacys about the time of the Conquest, and at one time one of the twelve baronial castles of the county stood hard by the town, not far from the parish church, and on the banks of what was then the course of the Irwell. This castle was in ruins at the time of the Civil War, when Bury was besieged by the Parliamentarians, and the remnants of the castle destroyed. Nothing now remains but a few stones which have been dug up from time to time, and a volunteers' armoury occupies the site. Some authorities contend that the name of the town arose from this castle, Byri signifying in Saxon a fortified place. Others fancy that Bury was a Roman station, but nothing has ever been brought to light to support that view. The history of the manor of Bury is unknown prior to the reign of Henry II. It was then, along with some adjoining manors, in the possession of John de Lacy. The family of Henry de Bury afterwards became owners of the lordship of Bury, and they were succeeded by the Pilkingtons, a family of some note in local records, whose residence in Leland's time was at Pilkington Park. Sir Thomas Pilkington was attainted after the fall of Richard III., by whom he stood, and his manors and possessions fell to the Stanleys as part reward for their services to Richmond. Since that time the manorial rights have remained with the Earls of Derby.

In the times antecedent to Henry VIII. the population of Bury was principally composed of such people as were needed about baronial residences, but when the feudal system died out the men of Bury began to better themselves in new forms of industry. The woollen manufacture was introduced by the Flemings in the fourteenth century, and it appears to have flourished greatly for the two succeeding centuries, being at a high point during the reign of Good Queen Bess. At a later period, when cotton spinning became a Lancashire industry, it was largely taken up by Bury people, and the woollen trade was allowed to some extent to drop. The nearness of Bury to Manchester, with the excellent supplies which it possessed of water and coal, made it peculiarly adapted for the purposes of carrying on the cotton industry, and from a very early period in the history of that manufacture Bury has occupied a prominent position therein. Several important improvements in the cotton manufacture had their origin in Bury. John Kay, a native of the town, invented a new method of throwing the shuttle by means of the picking peg instead of by the hand, which was called the fly shuttle; and in 1760 Robert Kay, his son, invented the drop box, by means of which the weaver could at will use any one of three shuttles, an arrangement which made it almost as easy to produce a fabric of different colours as a common cloth of only one. Whitehead, postmaster of Bury in 1791, devoted his leisure to the same subject and invented a system of "piecing" the ends of the perpetually breaking threads.

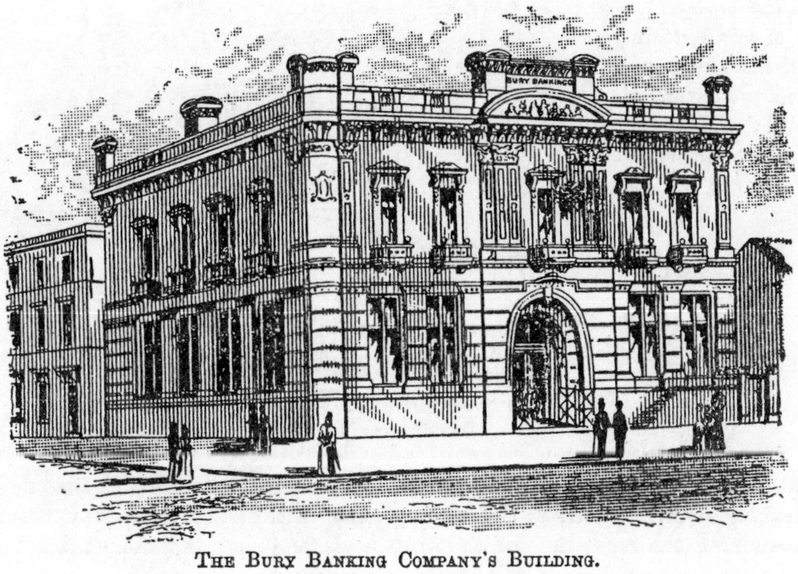

THE BURY BANKING COMPANY'S BUILDING.

A very large amount of the prosperity of Bury is due to the establishment by the first Sir Robert Peel of an extensive print works on the banks of the Irwell. Here he conducted a very important industry with an energy and enterprise which made it one of the most successful in the county. Sir Robert resided at Chamber Hall, and here his son, who was afterwards to become famous as a Prime Minister of England, was born. It is unnecessary to enter upon an examination of the career of that illustrious man, or to defend his conduct with regard to the Corn Laws, with which his fame will always be connected; but he was well worthy of the honour in which he was held by his fellow-citizens, who erected a bronze statue to his memory in the year 1851, just after his death. This statue is one of the ornaments of the town. To the impetus given by such men as Peel the trade and industry of Bury owe much, for their example was soon followed, and spinning and weaving became in a very short time one of the most important trades in the town. Mills were erected on every hand, every new improvement that experience or science could suggest in the way of better machinery or saving of labour was adopted by those at the head of affairs, and although Bury did not escape the contagion at the time when the introduction of machinery gave rise to so much opposition and ill-feeling, the men of the town soon came to see that after all these things were working together for their good, and bringing them increased work instead of reducing it. So they went on with the work in a hearty manner, and at the present moment the mills of Bury hold their own with those of any town in the county, not even excepting those of Manchester itself, both by reason of the quality of the goods produced and the quantity annually turned out, which mounts up to a very surprising total. In common with most Lancashire towns, Bury suffered somewhat severely at the time of the cotton famine, but those bad times are long since forgotten, and in the constant and busy hum of the machinery of to-day the contented and prosperous workers forget the hardships that are past.

In addition to the very important establishments devoted to the cotton spinning and weaving industries, and which employ the larger proportion of the inhabitants, Bury can boast a number of other manufactures, important in themselves and calculated to make the name of the town well known in the markets of the world. Excellent greystone quarries and coal mines are adjacent to the town, and have been worked with much profit for a number of years, the greystone being especially favoured by consumers, and the coal being largely required for local purposes. Large foundries and engine-works are also to be found in the town and its vicinity, devoted, as a matter of course, mainly to the production of such machinery as may be needed in the various industrial establishments of the town. The glare of many furnaces can e seen in various directions, and the Cyclopean labours are going on both early and late, the brawny and stout-chested engineers and blacksmiths adding a sturdy contingent to the men of Bury. Paper-making is also conducted in several large establishments. Lancashire paper enjoys a very great share of popular favour in all parts of England, and the handsomely-equipped factories to be seen in Bury are well to the fore in sustaining the reputation which has been acquired in the past. They are fitted with the most improved machinery, and employ a number of workmen. Bleaching, printing, and dye-works are also important features in the industrial life of Bury, and in these, as in all other departments, the greatest energy and enterprise are shown by all concerned As a matter of course, such a large community as this (it numbered 34,954 in 1829, and 49,476 in 1881) requires a considerable amount of supplies in the shape of food and clothing; and the handsome establishments which line the principal streets show that in this important respect all classes of society are well catered for.

So far as can be gathered from contemporary records Bury was not always the neat and well-kept town it now is. We find it recorded in 1836 that "the streets are now lighted with gas, and more attention is now paid than formerly to the cleansing and paving of the streets." "There are," says the same authority, "no waterworks, bu the inhabitants are well supplied with water by means of pumps." This sort of supply may have seemed very satisfactory to the scribe of half a century since, but it by no means suited the inhabitants of Bury, and one of the earliest things they turned their attention to was the obtaining of a good water-supply. After some time this was brought to pass, and the town is now in the possesssion of as good a supply as could possibly be wished. At that time the public officers of the town consisted of three constables, who were appointed at a court leet held at Whitsuntide, summoned by the Earl of Derby as Lord of the Manor, under whom a deputy-constable did the work. As the town grew in importance these primitive arrangements went by the board, and after passing through the usual stages the crowning triumph of municipal work was achieved by the obtaining of a charter of incorporation. This was in the year 1876, and it was a proud day for the good people of Bury when the all-important parchment was received in the town. A mayor and corporation were elected in all due formality, and municipal life has quickened in a remarkable degree from that time, the representatives of the ratepayers being actuated by the greatest possible anxiety to do the best they can for the town they have seen grow up around them. Bad paving and defective cleansing are things of the past now, and wherever possible endeavours have been made to secure broad and well-lighted thoroughfares in place of the narrow and ill-paved wynds which did duty in a former generation. The gas and water supply has been well looked after, and the wants of residents in the matter of reading-rooms and recreation grounds adequately supplied. A handsome Town Hall and Athenæum form part of a splendid block of buildings adjoining the Derby Hotel, the principal one in the town, to the erection of which the Earl largely contributed. There are also a Chamber of Commerce, mechanics' and other institutes, Liberal and Conservative clubs, several handsome bank buildings, a public market, and a number of other local institutions.

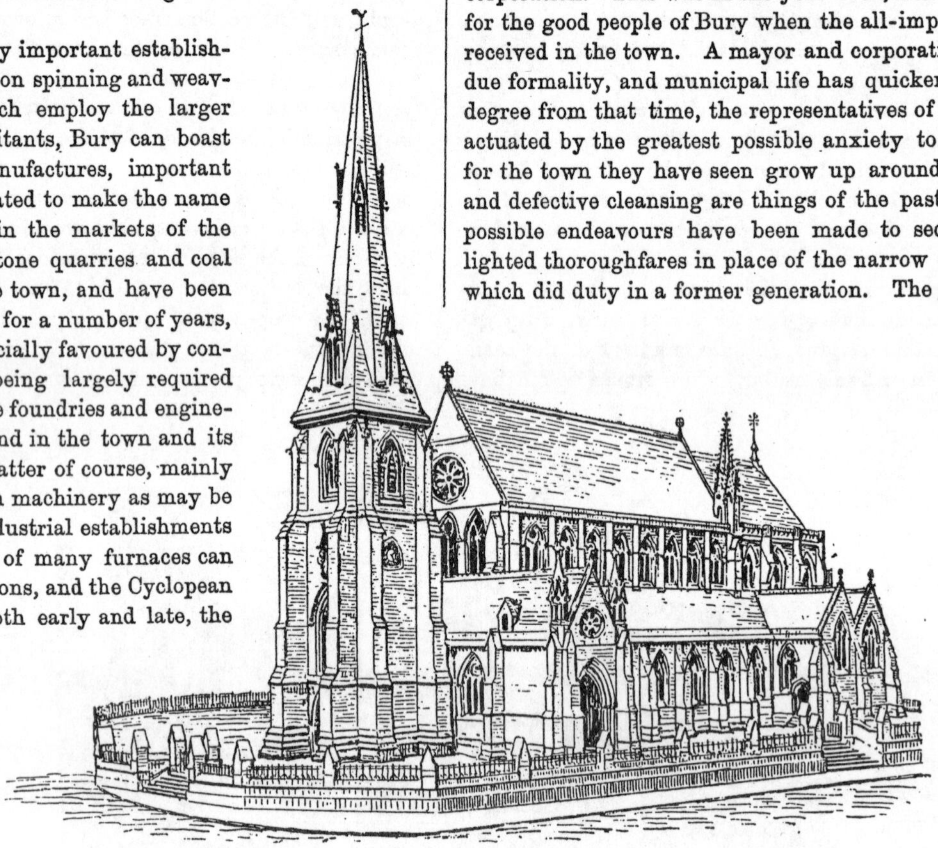

Bury Parish Church.

The parish church of Bury is dedicated to St. Mary, and the original building was probably of ancient date, seeing that it is mentioned by old writers as adjacent to the castle already mentioned. It was rebuilt in 1776 all but the steeple, and a hundred years later the edifice was again reconstructed, the result being that it is now one of the finest in the whole of Lancashire. The tower and spire remain as they were rebuilt in 1843. The living of St. Mary is a rectory in the deanery of Manchester, and the patron is Lord Derby. At one time the glebe land formed nearly one-half of the town, and in 1764 an Act of Parliament was passed empowering the rector to grant leases of the land for 99 years renewable at any time. St. John's Church is a neat building; and there are other churches devoted to the Establishment, as well as a number of Nonconformist churches and chapels, with their supplemental schools and societies. The Roman Catholics have also a chapel and schools.

In addition to the establishments for the education of the young provided by the School Board and voluntary schools, there is an excellent Grammar School situate near the church. This school

The Athenæum, Bury.

was founded by one Roger Kay in the year 1726, and endowed with certain estates. It was reorganized in the year 1861, and is now managed by trustees. The subjects embraced in the curriculum are classics, mathematics, modern languages, drawing, science, and English subjects, and there are two exhibitions tenable at either of the Universities. The fees range from four to eight guineas per annum; but formerly they were one pound in the upper school and ten shillings in the lower per annum. A charity school was founded for girls in 1748 by the Hon. and Rev. John Stanley, and in 1815 this was converted into a National School.

Bury is a Parliamentary borough returning one member to the House of Commons. It has had this honour since 1832, and it is at present represented by the Right Hon. Sir Henry James, who was returned unopposed at the general election of 1886. Sir Henry James is a Liberal Unionist.

One of the most interesting events which has occurred of late years in connection with the history of Bury was the opening, in July of last year (1888), of the Rochdale Road Recreation Ground by His Royal Highness Prince Albert Victor, eldest son of the Prince and Princess of Wales. For many years previously the necessity for some such place as this had been continuously urged in the columns of the local press and elsewhere, and after a considerable amount of discussion and negotiation it was finally decided, at a town meeting held in August, 1885, that the idea of purchasing land for a park should be abandoned for the present, and that £10,000, which Lord Derby had generously offered to deduct from the price of any land that might be purchased, should be utilised in the purchase of sites for the formation of three recreation grounds of seven acres each, situate in Manchester, Walmersley, and Rochdale Roads. A public subscription was also opened, and a large amount collected. The Rochdale Road site having been selected, the committee were gratified at receiving a notification from Mr. T. O. Openshaw that he would present the town with five acres of land adjoining and pay the expense of laying it out as a pleasure ground and gymnasium. This munificent offer was subsequently supplemented by the sum of £5,000 as an endowment for the ground, Mr. Openshaw's gift to the town being thus equal to about £15,000. The ground was at once laid out in a tasteful and ornamental manner and formed into a veritable park for that portion of the town situate on the banks of the Roach, and presenting a very pleasant appearance. The consent of Prince Albert Victor to open this and the other grounds having been obtained, every preparation was made for a gala day, and on Saturday, July 21st, the great event duly came to pass, everything going off in the most successful manner. The town was gaily decorated and the utmost enthusiasm was shown by all concerned.

View in Recreation Grounds, Bury.

No reference to the history and progress of Bury would be complete without a reference to the Volunteer movement, which has reached in this town a point and degree of importance which have made it famous in all parts of the kingdom, and which have formed the subject of a very interesting work by Mr. T. H. Hayhurst. From the information so carefully collated by this author, it would seem that the idea of volunteering as we understand it now was first suggested in Bury towards the middle of the seventeenth century, when the north of England was sore troubled by the Scots, who had taken Newcastle, and were threatening other towns. "Then," says an ancient letter written by a member of the Dunster family and quoted by Mr. Hayhurst, "was England in a fright for she did not knowe what to doe, but att last all the freehoulders and trayned bande weare caled togather every hundred by itselfe and trayned for a fortnight togather also all betwixt 16 and 60 weare caled togather so that upon the 8th of 7ber being Bury fayre there was at Burye 40 thousand with such weapons as ye could gett and these that had no better took euery one a great clubb and it was called Clubb Fayre at Burye and all the provision for the fayre was eaten uppe that daye. So that ye 800 which trayned there were scanted for a fortnight after of vituals the Duchess and Allewynes made a gayme of them. Then great troups of souldiers weare sent into Yorkshire and it was thought that there wd have been some bataylespeedely But the Lord turned all to peace." The Scots went home again, having made a compact with the Long Parliament for the sum of three thousand pounds as travelling expenses; and thus was inaugurated a feeling of military ardour which seems never to have died out in Bury. "Dulce et decorum est pro patriâ mori" is a fine old crusted quotation, but Bury folk believe in it thoroughly and have given many proofs of their faith in the ways of association and preparation. Reverting to the early history of the movement, it would seem that when Lord Strange, seventh Earl of Derby, was Lord-Lieutenant of the county, the news of the Protestant massacres in Ireland sent a thrill of horror through Lancashire, and caused a gathering together for self-defence. Lord Strange, who resided at Bury, became a volunteer, and a magazine of arms was formed in the town. Later on, when the troubles between King and Parliament reached an acute stage, Bury had plenty to occupy its attention, notable volunteers from the neighbourhood being Lord Strange, Captain Holt, of Bridge Hall, and Ralph Assheton; the first two on the King's side, and the latter that of the Parliament.

YOUNG MEN'S CHRISTIAN ASSOCIATION'S NEW BUILDINGS, BURY.

Of the exciting events of the period it is unnecessary to say anything, save that they found the Lancashire men steady and resolute and brave whether they fought on the side of the King or espoused the cause of those who claimed to represent the people. It was in 1798 that the Government of the day began to recognise the position of volunteer forces, and at that time a corps was formed in Bury by and with the active approval of Mr. Robert Peel, whose name was one to conjure with in Bury and its vicinity. This corps was formed under his supervision, and was known as the Bury Loyal Association of Volunteers. It was a grand day for Bury when this company went out for the first time in all the pomp and panoply of their brand new uniforms; but the feeling which attended the men who formed that association has been handed down from father to son, and nowhere in the kingdom has the volunteer movement been more successful than here. As is well known, the formation of Volunteer Corps on a large scale was commenced in 1859, and it is worthy of note that the official document in which Government sanction was announced was signed by General Peel, a native of Bury, who was at that time Secretary of State for War. Bury was one of the first to take advantage of the permission accorded, and in a very short time the 8th Lancashire Rifle Volunteers became an accomplished fact. How it has progressed and multiplied since that date, how men like Colonel Hutchinson have worked day and night to make it a model corps, how its example has been followed by other corps, and how it has attained to a point of efficiency second to none, is not all this written in the local records, too lengthily to be further referred to here?

An important organization in Bury is the Young Men's Christian Association, which is undenominational and non-political. The foundation stones of the present building were laid in May, 1888, by the Mayoress (Mrs. Horridge) and Sir Henry James, M.P., and the public opening took place on February 26, of the present year, 1889. Messrs. Maxwell and Tuke were the contractors, and Mr. J. Comfort the architect. The accommodation provided includes lecture-rooms, reading-rooms, gymnasium, library, &c. Mr. Samuel Knowles, M.P., is President of the Institution, and the Secretary is Mr. W. G. Wood. The Y.M.C.A. is highly esteemed by the residents in the borough, and has a very large muster-roll.

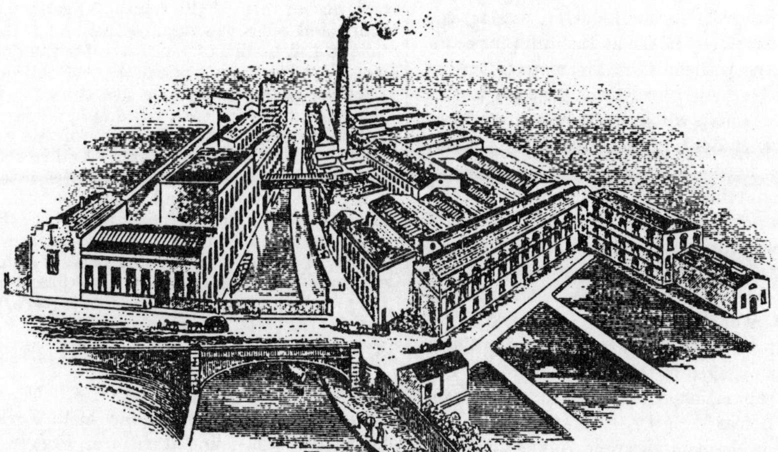

Messrs. J. R. Crompton & Bros., Elton Paper Mills, Bury, Lancashire.—Of the many large industrial establishments which have spread the name and fame of Lancashire to all parts of the civilised world, there are few which exceed in interest or influence the extensive works of Messrs. J. R. Crompton and Bros., Manufacturers of white and coloured tissue papers, &c., the Elton Paper Mills, Bury. This gigantic business was originally established early in the present century, and was carried on at the Kearsley Paper Works, Stoneclough, near Bolton, by the late Mr. Roger Crompton, with whom was the late Mr. James Roger Crompton. On the death of the former gentleman these works were disposed of, and the late Mr. J. R. Crompton commenced the Elton Paper Works at Bury in the year 1856. This gentleman (the father of the present proprietors) died in the year 1874, and for thirteen years the business was carried on by his executors, under the management of the sons, when in 1887, the firm assumed its present title. The Elton Paper Mills are very extensive and well arranged; the buildings are situated on the bank of the River Irwell, the Manchester, Bolton, and Bury Canal running almost through the centre of them, and forming a convenient waterway for the economical conveyance of coal, raw material, &c., to the Works. The buildings and roadways on each side of the canal are connected by substantial bridges, and the whole of the works are constructed with a special regard to the saving of labour. The large warehouses recently built at great expense, for the storage of raw materials, are of the best fireproof construction, and these buildings, together with those for the first processes of sorting, dusting, cutting, and boiling the rags, &c., are situated on the opposite side of the canal to the larger portion of the works, so that in case of fire it is impossible for the whole premises to be destroyed. The water, which is such an important essential in the manufacture of paper, is supplied from three large reservoirs situated about three-quarters of a mile from the works, and from an artesian well on the premises. An additional supply is obtained from the river Irwell, and is pumped up into a large reservoir adjoining the works by a powerful centrifugal pump, capable of lifting three thousand gallons a minute. This water is afterwards filtered through a number of sand and gravel filters covering a large area. These three independent sources for obtaining a water supply comprise a very valuable water-right, for in case one supply gives out there are always two to fall back upon, and even in the dryest seasons the works have never been stopped for want of water. The various departments are replete with the most modern machinery and appliances, embodying all the latest improvements and the most comprehensive utilities, no expense being spared by the proprietors, whose object has always been to be ahead of the times, and to manufacture their particular classes of paper on thoroughly scientific principles. The motive power for the machinery is supplied by no less than twelve steam engines by such eminent makers as Messrs. Yates, of Blackburn, Walmsley, Bentley and Jackson, and Kay, of Bury, and other equally well-known paper makers' engineers and machinists. There are also nine steam boilers made by different firms in the district, consuming upwards of a thousand tons of coal per month. The works contain six paper-making machines of various widths, with all the necessary preparatory plant for bleaching, washing, beating. and dyeing the pulp. There are also quite a number of glazing calenders, cutting, reeling, and embossing-machines, &c., &c., all of which are of the best and most modern construction. The sorting and making-up departments are very capacious. Here a large number of girls are employed, who have to examine each sheet separately, the best and perfect paper being packed in reams as of fit quality for the market at full market price, the spotted sheets and less perfect are made up in reams and marked xx or "retree," and are of considerably lower value, but, comparatively speaking, little of this latter quality reaches the market, so perfect are the arrangements, so skilful are the workmen, and so careful the superintendence of the various processes. In regard to the papers manufactured by this eminent firm, firstly may be mentioned coloured tissues, in which they so far excel all other makers. The brilliancy and variety of the colours are marvellous, there being upwards of two hundred shades, from the lightest to the darkest, almost every conceivable tint being included in their sample book. These papers are certainly very beautiful both in texture and delicacy of colour, their regularity and freedom from spots and lumps is as remarkable as their variety of shade and brilliancy of colour. The firm manufacture also white tissues of four qualities, cream shade, French white and blue shade; also copying-papers, glazed and unglazed, white, blue shade, buff, and yellow cigarette papers, of all kinds, plain, laid, and ribbed. These are of exceptional purity and quality. "Grass-bleached" tissue for silver and plated goods, &c.; imitation Japanese tissues in three qualities; "Perfection" stereotyping tissue; tracing papers in rolls and reams; "Perfection" manifold paper, free from oil; coloured 9 lb. double crown in two qualities; "Perfection" toilet paper in rolls and packets; waxed tissues; thick grease-proof papers, waterproof, air-proof, and damp-proof—these are excellent substitutes for vegetable parchment, &c. In the production of these papers the highest skill as well as the best raw material is requisite. These papers are known to the trade all over the world by the "Dog" trade mark and "Mill No. 39;" every ream being labelled with these distinctive marks, which are looked upon as a guarantee of quality. As an additional precaution, many of the papers are also water-marked. It is no uncommon thing for the firm to receive orders for "Dog" tissue, hence the origin of their abbreviated telegraphic address, "Dog-Paper, Bury." The whole of the works cover fully four acres of ground, and are lighted throughout by electricity; and a large number of hands being regularly employed, they at all times, night and day, present a busy and animated scene of industrial activity. The offices are fitted with speaking-tubes to the various departments, and are connected by telephone with the Bury Centre and the Manchester Exchange. The mercantile department is conducted in a spacious suite of well-appointed offices, in which quite an army of clerks, correspondents, and assistants are actively engaged in the various clerical duties appertaining to this branch of the business. There are also three handsomely-furnished apartments on the first-floor exclusively for the use of the principals. The present partnership comprises Mr. James R. Crompton, Mr. Ralph Crompton, and Mr. Percy R. Crompton. All these gentlemen take an active part in the business, and occupy prominent and influential positions in social and mercantile circles. Mr. Percy Crompton, having studied chemistry and the art of dyeing, gives his sole personal attention to this most important part of the business. He has a well-appointed laboratory adjoining the offices, and every chemical and dye used on the premises is accurately analysed and tested by him or his assistant chemist. It will thus be seen that this firm has exceptional facilities for manufacturing special kinds of paper that require extraordinary skill and scientific and chemical knowledge, that only long experience and close attention to business can give. We believe it is a fact that this firm will undertake to match in paper any colour that has been dyed in cotton, woollen, or silk goods, and we know that the colours they have produced and are producing every day are such as have never before been obtained or attempted in paper. The business connections are of a wide-spread, influential, and steady-growing character, and extend to all parts of the world; and in their particular line Messrs. J. R. Crompton & Bros. are the largest manufacturers, either in this or any other country. The firm have warehouses and offices at Queenhithe, London, and at 8, Sussex Street, Manchester, and 99, West Nile Street, Glasgow, besides extensive connections in France, where they obtained prize medals at the Paris Exhibition of 1867 and 1878. They also have a large business connection in America. It is particularly interesting, in writing an historical notice of the commerce and industries of Bury and the district, to meet with an establishment of such old standing and extensive connections, and to accord to this eminent firm that special prominence in these reviews which its influential position in the trade so justly demands.

James Wrigley & Son, Limited, Paper Makers, Bridge Hall Mills, Bury; 29, John Dalton Street, Manchester; and 21, Budge Row, London, E.C.—There is probably no industry, among the many which have been extensively developed in Great Britain, that occupies a more thoroughly representative position than the manufacture of paper; and among the various notable Lancashire firms engaged in this branch of productive enterprise there is none whose name is better known than that of Messrs. James Wrigley & Son, Limited, of Bury. Established as far back as the year 1813, by the grandfather of the present principals, this house has always maintained a position of eminence and distinction in the paper trade. Its prosperity as a commercial concern has been steady, continuous, and substantial throughout a long career, and its history embodies in epitomized form the most interesting records of paper-making, as comprised in the wondrous development of that industry during the last three-quarters of a century. Mr. James Wrigley was the founder of the house, and at the time of his commencement as a paper-maker at Bridge Hall Mills he engaged in the manufacture of both hand and machine-made papers, in connection with which his name soon became a noted one. His son, Mr. Thomas Wrigley, succeeded him in the control of the business, and under his able and vigorous *régime* the house attained the place of prominence in the trade which it has ever since so well and so worthily occupied. As a public controversialist and an able expounder of many vexed questions of popular importance, Mr. Thomas Wrigley is perhaps as well known by reputation to the people as he was to the trade in his commercial capacity. Those whose memory holds a good impress of the happenings of thirty years ago will be sure to recollect his series of six trenchant and thoughtful letters to the *Times* on the subject of the Customs duty on foreign paper; and again, in further connection with the paper trade, his pamphlet on the "Paper Trade considered with reference to its Material," was much read and admired for its able defence of the British paper-makers, who were at that time regarding with some apprehension the effect and possibilities of the Act of Parliament concerning the Customs duty above referred to. Mr. Wrigley, furthermore, became a recognised authority on railway signalling and the means of preventing railway accidents, with which subjects he dealt at length in four other interesting and readable pamphlets. Finally, his written views and expressions of opinion on the education of the people must be accorded a place among the most thoughtful and practical of the host of treatises issued in various forms during the last thirty-five years, on the great and absorbing problem of effective popular education. Gifted with the capacity to think deeply as well as with the energy and force of character essential to prompt and vigorous action, it is not surprising that Mr. Thos. Wrigley should have made a high mark among notable Lancashire men of his time. He was, in 1870, chosen High Sheriff of the county. His death occurred in January, 1880. He has been succeeded by his three sons, Mr. Edwin Grundy Wrigley (chairman of the present Company), Mr. Oswald Osmond Wrigley, and Mr. Frederick Wrigley. Messrs. Oswald and Frederick Wrigley are justices of the peace for the county of Lancashire. The private limited company, under which constitution the business is now carried on, was formed in 1884, the principals comprising the three gentlemen just named, some of the heads of departments in Bury, Manchester, and London; and upon these new lines of organisation the house has been more successful, if that be possible, than ever before. Messrs. James Wrigley & Son, Limited, have long maintained a standard reputation for the fine quality and excellent finish of all their manufactures in paper of various kinds; and so substantial is this reputation at the present day that the productions of the house can well dispense with anything resembling advertisement. The firm's specialities may, however, be briefly enumerated here, and will be found to comprise the following:—Superfine, fine, and all other grades of printings; music and plate papers; various qualities of account-book papers; lithographic and plate-glazed printings; laid and wove writings, in a large assortment of tints; plain and lettered cheque papers; white and tinted ivory boards for high-class work; map and drawing papers, cartridge papers, and blottings; antique etching papers; antique printings; all grades of cream-laid and cream-wove writings; super-callendered papers; super-vellum laid and wove papers; and all qualities of news papers in reams or in web, the firm being one of the makers for the *Times* (London). Of these goods the firm made a remarkable display at the Manchester Exhibition of 1887, where they gained high honours, and where their unique stand formed a constant centre of attraction for all classes of visitors. Messrs. Wrigley's mills at Bury cover upwards of eight acres of ground, including the area occupied by the comfortable cottages of the workpeople, and the staff employed numbers fully six hundred hands. This fact alone will afford some indication of the magnitude of the industry, when it is borne in mind that the mills are equipped throughout with plant and machinery of the most effective modern type. There are no fewer than eleven highly improved paper-making machines regularly at work in the Bridge Hall Mills, and the annual output of the establishment in papers of all kinds and qualities is enormous. The trade at the house is of world-wide extent, and its operations are directed with admirable energy and judgment by the present principals of the concern. Mr. Edwin Grundy Wrigley, the head of the firm, has been an indefatigable business man since he commenced his commercial career, forty years ago. He is in almost constant attendance at one or other of the firm's establishments—in Bury, or at Manchester or London and he has infused the spirit of his own untiring energy into everything connected with the administration of the house. He is a deputy-lieutenant and justice of the peace for the county palatine of Lancaster, and is well known as a staunch and influential supporter of the Liberal Unionist cause, though he has thus far refrained from the contesting of any parliamentary seat, preferring to devote his energies continuously to the development and promotion of the great business in which he has so long been actively interested. And in this work it is hardly necessary to add that he is loyally seconded and assisted by his capable partners in the firm, Messrs. Oswald and Frederick Wrigley. Messrs. James Wrigley & Son, Limited, have an important establishment at 29, John Dalton Street, Manchester; and their fine London warehouse in Budge Row, Cannon Street, is one of the most extensive, commodious, and convenient in the metropolitan paper trade. The firm's mill number is 219, and their telegraphic addresses are—"Wrigleys, Bury," "Wrigleys, London," and "Wandson, Manchester."

Frederick Smith & Co., Manufacturers of Tobacco, Snuff, and Cigars, Virginia Mill, York Street, Bury.—This representative and well-founded business was established by Mr. Frederick Smith in 1864, who commenced in a very small way in Stanley Street, Bury, but gradually developed his trade until larger premises were necessary. In 1870, in order to meet this requirement, Mr. Smith removed to Bolton Street, remaining there for a period of fourteen years. These premises, however, were also found inadequate, and the building of the Virginia Mill was entered upon; no expense was spared in order to make this a first-class tobacco factory. The building is 75 feet by 35 feet, with a large yard at the rear, upon which, if necessary, another mill may be built to meet the requirements of this pushing firm. Altogether a space of about 750 yards is occupied at present. Mr. Smith still retains as a retail establishment the premises in Bolton Street, where formerly the tobacco, &c., was manufactured. In their manufacture of tobacco, snuff, and cigars, Messrs. Frederick Smith & Co. are aided by powerful machinery of the very latest and most approved construction. There are two horizontal engines by C. Walmsley, of Bury, and one horizontal boiler,

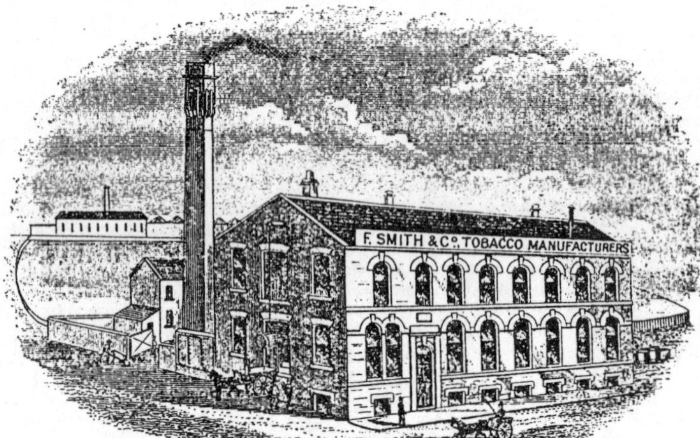

MESSRS. F. SMITH AND CO.'S TOBACCO FACTORY, BURY, LANCASHIRE.

14 feet by 5½ feet. Messrs. Frederick Smith & Co. make a speciality of their flake cavendish, which they largely advertise by handsome coloured show-cards, to be met with everywhere. At present thirty hands are employed, but the improved machinery of the firm enables them to dispense with a large number of employés, who, with less modern appliances, would be necessary in the conduct of this business. The basement floor is devoted to the process of tobacco cutting, and is furnished with two tobacco-cutting machines—one by Garnett & Moore, of Liverpool, and the other by Robert Legg, of London. Here also is the snuff mill, where the snuff is ground and roasted. There are here, also, presses for the making of twist tobacco. The ground floor contains the private offices, saleroom, and general office, forming handsome parts of the structure. Beyond the saleroom is a large room of about 60 feet square used as the "leaf-room." On the second floor is the spinning-room. A great proportion of the spinning is done by hand, a certain amount being also performed by patent machinery put in by Messrs. Andrews, of Stockport. Cigar making is also conducted on the same floor. Two travellers cover Lancashire ground, but a good business is also transacted in various parts of England. This is a concern most energetically conducted, highly popular, and much respected.

Messrs. Joshua Hoyle & Sons, Limited, Brooksbottoms Mills, Summerseat, near Bury.—An old mill worked by John Robinson Kay, Esq., as a spinning and manufacturing concern formerly occupied

PLANTATION MILL, BACUP.

the ground on which the present magnificent Brooksbottom Mills, Summerseat, are built. This old building was removed in 1873, and the new one commenced by Messrs. Joshua Hoyle & Sons, Limited. The structure was completed in 1875, and the spinning and weaving commenced the year following. The premises are as substantial and handsomely built as any mills in the district, and for completeness in all the details necessary to the equipment of a large manufacturing concern the Brooksbottoms Mills are not surpassed by any other similar establishment in Lancashire. The entire block is stone built, of massive, though extremely elegant proportions, admirably constructed and well arranged, both with respect to economy in working and the health and comfort of the numerous employés. The main building is four storeys high, in addition to which there are two immense weaving sheds, built in five divisions. In addition to an adequate amount of preparatory machinery and appliances, embodying all the latest improvements and most comprehensive utilities, the mill contains 42,000 spindles, the mules being made by Messrs. Dobson & Barlow, of Bolton, and the throstles by Mr. John Mason, of Rochdale. The motive power for this portion of the works is communicated from two splendid beam engines of over 800 h.-p. and six Lancashire boilers, made by Petrie,

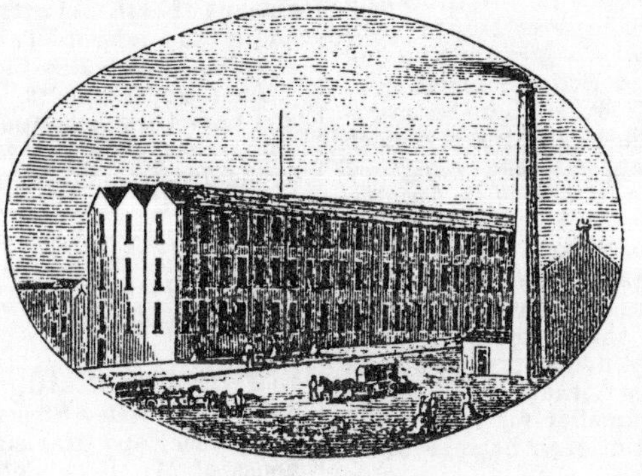

BEECH MILL, BACUP.

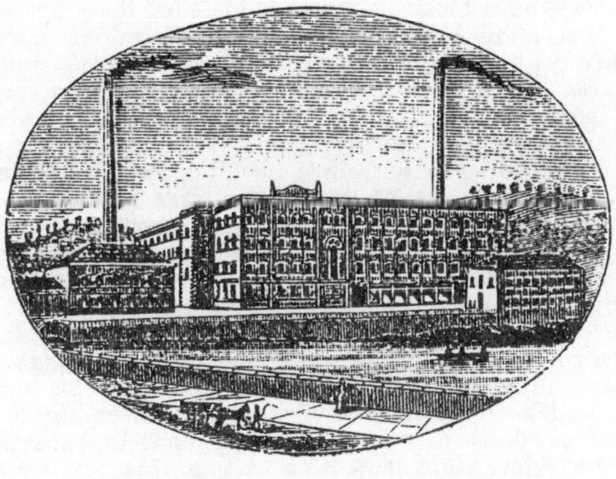

BROOKSBOTTOMS MILL, SUMMERSEAT.

of Rochdale. The ground floor of the mill is used for carding and general preparation purposes, and the higher storeys are occupied by the spinning machinery. In the weaving department there are 1,401 looms, made by Messrs. Butterworth & Dickenson, of Burnley. The No. 2 shed is worked by two beam engines each of 160 ind. h.-p., made by Petrie, of

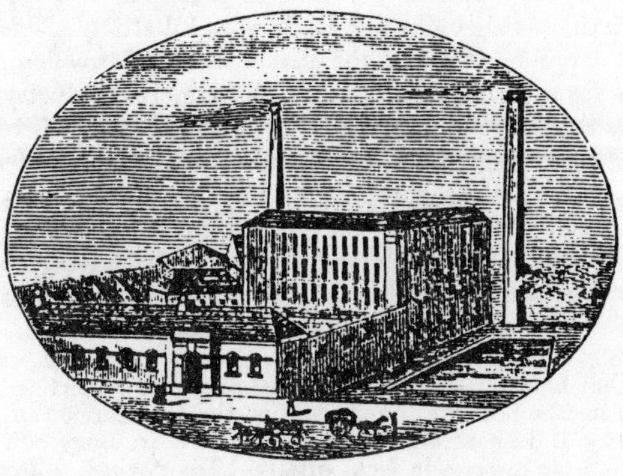

INDIA MILL, BACUP.

Rochdale, and the three boilers, of the Lancashire type, are by the same firm. The machinery in the No. 5 shed, which is much smaller, is worked by one horizontal engine of 120 ind. h.-p.; made by Petrie, of Rochdale, and the two Lancashire boilers are made by Petrie and W. and J. Galloway & Sons, Manchester. Messrs. Joshua Hoyle & Sons, Limited, have also very extensive spinning and manufacturing establishments at Bacup (1,601 looms and 54,000 spindles), known as the Plantation, India, and Beech Mills, and Freeholds Mill, Shawforth. At the Brooksbottoms Mill alone the firm employ 850 hands. It is not often that picturesque associations of scenery and manufacturing industry are so happily united as here, for the Brooksbottoms Mills at Summerseat are situated amidst some of the most lovely scenery in Lancashire. The Manchester warehouse of the firm is at No. 41, Mosley Street, where they hold a very large stock of goods fully representative of this branch of the cotton industry. Messrs. Joshua Hoyle & Sons, Limited, have a splendid business connection, extending to all parts of the United Kingdom, and also do a large and continually increasing export trade, being well represented in the Continental, American and Colonial markets, and the proprietors never for a moment relax their exertions to maintain and extend the high reputa-

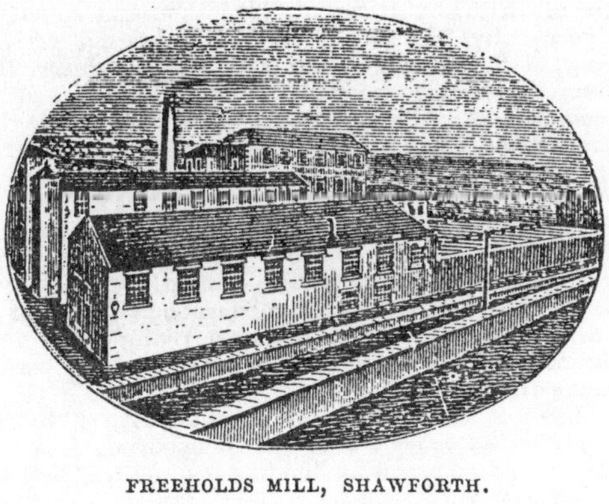

FREEHOLDS MILL, SHAWFORTH.

tion their goods have achieved when placed in competition with those of the manufacturers of this and other countries.

Geo. Chadwick & Co., Tanners, Bury Ground, Bury.—This firm was founded in 1870, and throughout the whole of its career has met with a more than usual amount of success, which may be justly attributed to the enterprise and ability with which it has been conducted. The works comprise premises that are very suitably adapted to the purposes of the trade, and include various rooms and departments, in which is fitted a large amount of machinery and plant incidental to this particular industry. The whole of the arrangements are upon the most modern and improved scale, and nothing has been omitted that may tend to render the premises thoroughly complete in every detail. The trade carried on is that of the tanner, a branch in which Mr. Chadwick has had many years' practical experience, and has a thoroughly sound knowledge of every branch. A large number of hands are employed in the various departments, all of which are under the supervision of the proprietor. The special feature of the work for which the firm is more particularly noted is the manufacture of oak-tanned picking straps, supplied to the various mill-owners, for drawing the shuttle in all classes of weaving. In this direction Mr. Chadwick has acquired a widespread reputation, and his firm is one of the best known in the trade. He is also noted for the manufacture of green leather packing-straps, which are exported in large quantities to all parts of the Continent, India, North and South America, and the Colonies generally. In all branches a very extensive business is done, and under the able and energetic direction of the proprietor great progress is still being made in all directions. Mr. Chadwick is widely known and respected, both socially and commercially, and has for many years been the manager of the Whitefield National Schools.

James Kenyon & Son, Derby Street Mills, Pilsworth Mills, and Roach Bank Mills, Bury; and **Crimble Mills,** Heywood.—The house of Messrs. James Kenyon & Son, founded in 1827 by the late Mr. James Kenyon, father of the present principal, is a representative institution in the textile industries of Bury and district. This firm have developed a large business in the manufacture of woollen, linen, and cotton cloths for machinery; and this is the principal industry carried on at the Derby Street Mills, Bury; and the Pilsworth and Crimble Mills. Blankets for calico printers; felts for paper makers, and roller cloths for cotton spinners, constitute specialities to which particular attention is given. At Roach Bank Mills the production of "plains," "stripes," "twills," and sateens, is largely engaged in; and the total working staff at the four mills number nine hundred and eighty hands. Messrs. James Kenyon & Son ship to all parts of the world, and trade extensively in the home markets. Their goods meet with general approval, and enjoy a reputation that has always been their best and only advertisement. Mr. James Kenyon, the head of the firm, is in the Commission of the Peace for the county of Lancaster, and is well known in Bury, where he has taken considerable interest in local affairs. He devotes a large portion of his time to the management of the extensive business that bears his name.

Horridge & Cornall, Bolholt Print Works, Bury; Warehouse, 28A, Faulkner Street, Manchester.—The Bolholt Print Works, at Bury, were established by Messrs. Sudren, the present proprietors being Messrs. Horridge & Cornall, who came into possession in 1871, this firm having previously carried on the same class of business at Mount Sion, Radcliffe. The Bolholt Print Works are fitted with a large engine and three boilers, the latter being made by Pollitt, of Bolton, Adamson, of Dukinfield, and Heywood & Co., of Radcliffe. There are here six printing machines and twelve hand blocking machines, as also seventeen small engines. Messrs. Horridge & Cornall are very extensively engaged as calico printers and indigo blue piece dyers, the latter branch forming a speciality in the business of the firm. The trade is of a very large export class, and the productions emanating from the Bolholt Print Works, of Bury, are consigned to various ports throughout the world. The trade conducted by Messrs. Horridge & Cornall is chiefly wrought on exportation lines. Mr. George Horridge, one of the partners, of Elton Lodge, Bury, is ex-mayor for the borough of Bury, and at present acts as an alderman and justice of the peace. Mr. Thomas Cornall, of Lake Hill, Bury, the other member of the firm, is a town councillor for Bury; and both gentlemen are largely recognised on account of their business capabilities and powers of civic administration.

George Clegg, Dearden Clough Mill, Edenfield, near Bury.—Many years ago, this mill was in the possession of Messrs. Porrit, Brothers & Austin (now of Stubbins' Vale Mills, Stubbins). It was afterwards occupied by Messrs. William and John Cronshaw, who were succeeded by the present proprietor. The old mill was destroyed by fire, and rebuilt in 1872. It contains five thousand spindles (making 4s. to 10s. yarn), by Messrs. Walker & Hacking, of Bury, and Taylor & Lang, of Staleybridge, the carding machinery throughout emanating from the establishment of William Tatham, of Rochdale. There is a complement of one hundred and thirty looms by various makers; a beam engine of one hundred and twenty horse-power indicated, by J. C. Kay, of the Phœnix Works, Bury; and boiler measuring 7 by 30, by Messrs. Walker & Hacking, of Bury. The mill is entirely stone built and has a thoroughly solid and commercial appearance, and reaches to a height of three storeys. The entrance to the premises is approached by passing down a decline from the Rochdale Road, on the left side from Shuttleworth to Edenfield. This neighbourhood is one of the most picturesque in Lancashire, and the Dearden Clough Mill forms a fine object of relief to the general surroundings. A working staff of nearly a hundred hands are employed at this establishment. Mr. George Clegg, in addition to being a most capable and respected man of business, holds a prominent position as a member of the Ramsbottom Local Board, the duties of which are discharged by him in a manner yielding the highest satisfaction to all concerned.

William Nabb, Chartered Accountant, 3, Old Market Place, Bury.—This gentleman commenced business about five years since, and is still the only accountant in the town certified by examination. His offices are on the first floor of a very handsome building, and are well fitted up with every requisite for the comfort and convenience of his numerous clients. Considering the short time he has been in business, Mr. Nabb has enjoyed a most encouraging share of practice. Thoroughly *au fait* in the profession, he can always give his clients the best advice, he is most careful and painstaking, and all his energies are devoted to the best interests of those who seek his counsel and services. Under such circumstances his business is undergoing steady and well-deserved extension. He acts as agent for the Equitable Fire Office, the Northern Assurance Company, the Sun Life Office, and the Law Guarantee Society, and through his practice and business connections is able to contribute materially to the aggregate transactions of all these well-known and flourishing associations.

Samuel Smethurst & Sons, Bleachers and Dyers, Woolfold, Bury.—One of the foremost firms of bleachers and dyers of indigo and fancy colours in cotton warps and bundles in Lancashire is that of Messrs. Samuel Smethurst & Sons, of Woolfold, whose business was founded about forty-five years ago by Mr. Samuel Smethurst, the father of the present principals, Messrs. William and James Smethurst. This important house is very extensively engaged in bleaching and dyeing operations, and the works at Woolfold cover an area of upwards of four acres of ground. They are equipped in the most complete manner, and have all the best modern machinery applicable to an industry of this kind. The boiler and engine plant is one of remarkable power and efficiency, there being seven boilers and twenty engines in the establishment, all by Charles Walmsley, of Elton, a famous engineering house of which Mr. James Smethurst is now the principal partner. To indicate the remarkable manner in which Messrs. Samuel Smethurst & Sons have advanced their business from very modest beginnings to its present large and important proportions, we may mention that the founder of the house commenced his operations as a dyer and bleacher with one vat in his garden, and the yarn he had to take several miles to and fro in a wheelbarrow, as occasion required. Energy, perseverance, and a solid determination to succeed have wrought the usual result in the case of this house, and at the present day Messrs. Smethurst have one of the best bleach and dye works in this part of Lancashire, employing about 150 hands, and keeping sixteen horses and lurries for the conveyance of goods to and from the various customers. As to their commercial reputation it may be fairly said to be second to none in this line of trade, and they are justly famous for their indigo specialities, to which they devote a large amount of care and attention. The trade is very extensive and important, and is done principally through the great shipping houses, trading to the Continent and the Levant. Messrs. Smethurst, under the style of "Smethurst Brothers," do a large and important business as wool brokers and have their headquarters for this department in Spring Street, Bury. Altogether, the house is one of the most prominent commercial concerns in the district, and its principals enjoy a large degree of public confidence and esteem. Mr. William Smethurst is the present mayor of Bury, and is also a justice of the peace for the borough, in which both he and his brother hold influential positions that have been fairly and honourably won by their integrity and straightforwardness alike in private and mercantile life.

J. E. Schofield, Wholesale Grocer and Provision Merchant, Knowsley Street, Bury.—A leading position in connection with the grocery and provision trades in Bury is held by the well-known house of Mr. J. E. Schofield, a representative and important concern, whose commercial history dates back over a period of more than a quarter of a century. The business was founded by Mr. Schofield; it has been developed steadily and substantially by him, and it still remains under his energetic management, having gained a position of much more than ordinary prominence in the trade it represents. Mr. Schofield's establishment is situated in Knowsley Street, and is of very considerable extent, comprising a well-built block, in which is included the proprietor's dwelling-house. The main building stands well back from the roadway, a large yard (always presenting a scene of great activity) lying between it and the street. This principal edifice is equipped in a very complete manner, and possesses every facility and convenience desirable in a large and comprehensive grocery and provision trade. There is new and highly effective machinery for grinding coffee, blending teas, and cleaning fruits; and in the warehouse proper Mr. Schofield always holds a very extensive stock, embracing teas, coffees, spices, pickles, tinned goods and preserves, fish, game, meat, fruits, soaps, and every other article usually found in a first-rate provision merchant's, grocers', or Italian warehouseman's establishment. In this stock may be noticed not a few of Mr. Schofield's own specialities, among which we may specially commend his celebrated dry soap, one of the most useful and economical of domestic cleansing preparations. Packet teas are another speciality of note, and in introducing them to his connection Mr. Schofield has been highly successful. He puts these excellent teas up in ¼lb., ½lb., and 1lb. packets, and they are having a very large and increasing sale in this popular form. Mr. Schofield, furthermore, does a very extensive business with shopkeepers in household flour, and is sole agent in Lancashire for Louis Dobblemann of Rotterdam, cigar manufacturer, whose well-known goods he supplies. In all cases the articles and commodities sold by this house are of unexceptional quality, and Mr. Schofield never lends his name or influence to help the sale of inferior goods. He employs a numerous and efficient staff of hands, and has several carts and lurries, with four horses, for which latter there is good stabling adjacent to the warehouse. These horses and lurries, with a number of drivers and vanmen, are always busy in delivery work, and their activity speaks for the flourishing condition of the business. Three travellers are kept constantly on the road, and Mr. Schofield also travels himself in the interests of the house. The trade controlled extends all over Lancashire and is increasing year by year, the establishment possessing the favour and confidence of a large and valuable connection. Mr. Schofield is well known as an honourable and straightforward business man, and of him it may truly be said that he has won his present successful position by dint of hard work and the observance of sound principles. He is deservedly esteemed by all who have dealings with him, commercial or otherwise.

Acts of Parliament

A few of the Acts of Parliament, of the type known as Local Acts, passed about a century ago. In the 1870's, 14 Acts affecting Bury came onto the Statute Book, followed by 17 in each of the next two decades. That's one every 23 days, and is an indication of the municipal and commercial activity of Bury when it was booming.

[40 & 41 VICT.] *The Bury and Tottington District Railway Act*, 1877. [Ch. clvii.]

CHAPTER clvii.

An Act for making a Railway from Bury to Tottington, with branches, in the county palatine of Lancaster. A.D. 1877.

[2d August 1877.]

[43 & 44 VICT.] *Bury and Tottington District Railway Act*, 1880. [Ch. iv.]

CHAPTER iv.

An Act to authorise the Bury and Tottington District Railway Company to raise additional Capital; and for other purposes. [29th June 1880.]

CHAPTER lxix.

An Act to authorise the Corporation of Bury to construct a connecting Railway between their Gasworks and the Lancashire and Yorkshire Railway and for other purposes. [4th July 1890.] A.D. 1890.

[47 & 48 Vict.] *Manchester Bury Rochdale and Oldham Steam Tramways Act*, 1884. [Ch. clxiv.]

CHAPTER clxiv.

An Act for incorporating and conferring powers on the Manchester Bury Rochdale and Oldham Steam Tramways Company. [28th July 1884.] A.D. 1884.

[51 & 52 Vict.] *Lancashire and Yorkshire Railway Act*, 1888. [Ch. cxl.]

CHAPTER cxl.

An Act for conferring further Powers on the Lancashire and Yorkshire Railway Company with relation to their Undertaking and to enable them to acquire the Undertaking of the Bury and Tottington District Railway Company and to confer further Powers on the Halifax High Level and North and South Junction Railway Company with respect to their Undertaking and for other purposes. [24th July 1888.] A.D. 1888.

The inventor of the flying shuttle, John Kay, was born in Bury in 1704, and for many years his statue surmounted the premises of Robert ("Bobby") Hall, known world-wide as a manufacturer of textile machinery. The statue was removed to Yorkshire when the works were demolished, but Kay Gardens in the town centre, with its commemorative monument, still remains.

Road works posed a problem for vehicular traffic a century ago as well as to-day!

Alas, the facade of the Derby Hotel and the Atheneum in Market Street has disappeared, although the Derby Hall survives, and the right hand side is still recognisable.

Samuel Cook & Co., Spring Manufacturers, &c., Victoria Works, Bury.—The founder of the well-known enterprise conducted by Messrs. Samuel Cook & Co., spring manufacturers, machine makers, and mill furnishers, at Victoria Works, Bury, was Mr. Samuel Cook, one of the most respected inhabitants of the district. This gentleman for many years occupied high public positions in the town. He acted as a justice of the peace for the borough, and had fulfilled the duties of alderman, and also served as mayor. This gentleman carried on business for several years as leading partner in the well-known firm of Cook, Hacking & Co., in the foundry now occupied as a weaving shed by Messrs. Wilson & Ingham, of this town. On severing con-

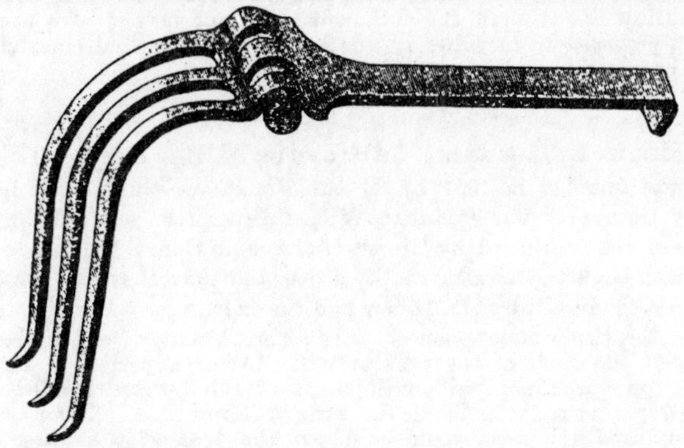

nection with this firm, Mr. Cook became connected in partnership with Mr. Hacking, the nephew of his former partner, when a most successful business was carried on by the firm as engineers, loom manufacturers, and machine makers. In 1862, the firm, which is now known as Samuel Cook & Co., became duly established, and after the death of Mr. Alderman Cook, his son, the present head of the firm, carried on the business of spring manufacturing with the most gratifying success, the firm taking a most perceptible "lead" in this branch of trade. Messrs.

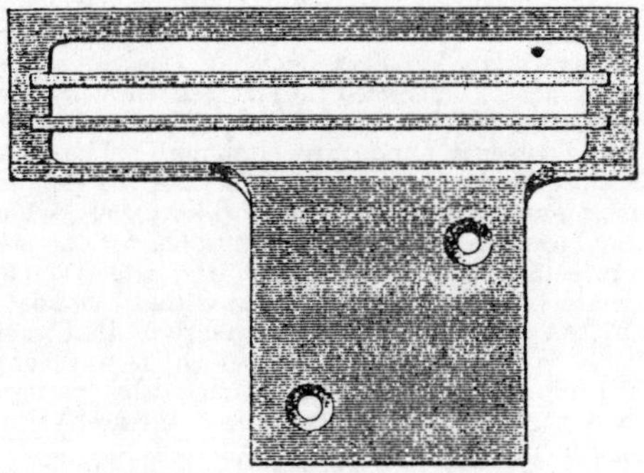

Samuel Cook & Co. also enjoy a wide reputation as heald and reed makers and mill furnishers generally. The buildings, which have a frontage of one hundred and fifty feet, recede in Back Foundry Street for a distance of seventy-six feet, and consist partly of two-floor and partly of three-floor erections. Much of this structure is quite new, the works having from time to time been re-constructed, enlarged, and improved. That portion of the block abutting on Back Foundry Street has only been completed within the past year or two. The machinery here is

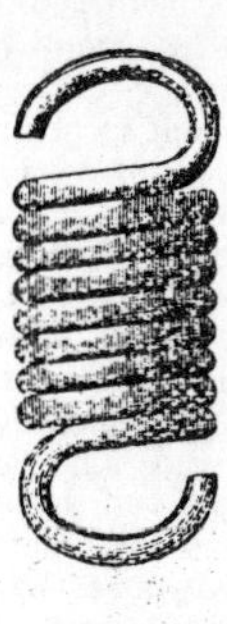

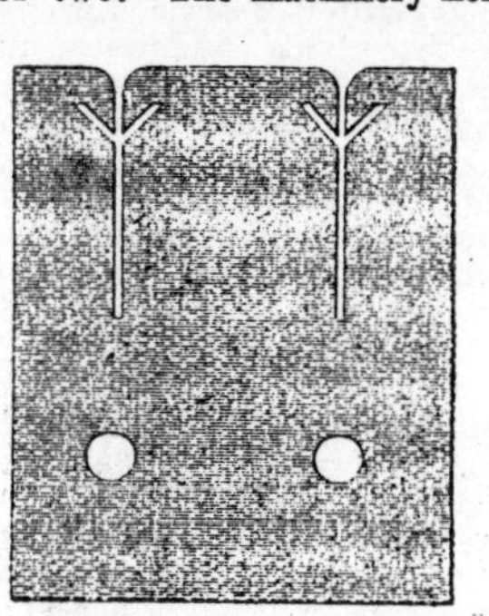

principally the construction of the firm, and it is not too much to say that more suitable appliances for the work engaged in could not be found in any engineering works in the country. With three engines of great collective power, a large amount of work is performed, and Messrs. Samuel Cook & Company are a firm fully aware as to how the business facilities they enjoy may be best utilised. The manufactures of this firm cover a wide field, and comprise back springs, swell springs, box end springs and spare studs, winding guides or yarn clearers, weft forks, weft grates, shuttle-box shelves, shuttle covers, underclearer and click springs, steel pattern cards, nippers, steel combs, &c., piston rings, expanding combs, spiral springs, patent metallic surfacing for taking up beams, healds, reeds, &c., &c. The most perfect order and system prevail throughout all the departments, and a staff of ninety hands are employed. On going over the offices, fitted up with every comfort and convenience, and through the various sections of this extensive concern, the visitor finds a plentiful indication of the thorough business capacity and energy of Mr. Samuel Cook, the present head of this most useful, valuable, and successful enterprise.

J. W. Worsley & Co., Hat Manufacturer, Bolholt Hat Works, Elton, Bury.—This important business was established in the present works in the year 1880, by Messrs. J. W. Worsley & Co., who are still the proprietors. Bolholt Works are of large extent, having a frontage of 120 feet, the buildings being of brick, and they are equipped in first-rate style with all the most approved machinery and appliances, and several important special appliances for turning out felt hats of every description. But the class of felts for which the house is best known in the trade are those for children in every shade of colour, and for this class the firm enjoys a high reputation in London, Manchester, and many foreign countries. Although a large business is done in England, this firm's trade is chiefly export, for which the firm's large warehouse and packing-room—where a large staff of hands are employed in addition to those in the manufactory—are admirably adapted. Mr. Worsley, the head of the firm, has long been well known in the trade, and he has won the well-deserved position he now enjoys through possessing a thorough practical knowledge of the business in all its details, hard work, and honourable methods in his management. Possessing an agreeable manner, and having a reputation for his upright principles, Mr. Worsley is much respected by all with whom he comes in contact in or out of business.

Charles Walmsley, Atlas Iron Works, Elton, Bury.—These iron works have been established over forty years, and the firm have just completed some extensive alterations in the workshop, and built a new fitting and erecting shop, making the establishment one of the most complete in the district. The speciality in the business is the production of pumping machinery for all purposes, and high-class automatic steam engines of every description and size up to 600 horse-power, for which they have established an important local and district reputation, the finish, durability, and workmanship being all that can be desired. The firm are also largely occupied in the production of machinery used in the paper manufacturing trade, and employ about 150 hands, who are at present busily engaged in the construction and erection of machinery for making wood pulp used by paper makers. Mill gearing and belt and rope pulleys up to 16 feet diameter are also extensively dealt with, and the firm also undertake to sink artesian wells or bore holes for water up to 30 inches diameter and 1,000 feet deep, and consequently pumps and engines for the same form a large portion of the business, as many of these undertakings are of great magnitude. The business is conducted by Mr. C. Walmsley, who is a man of sound practical knowledge and persevering business energy.

H. M. Dearden, Printer, &c., 31, Fleet Street, Bury.—This firm was founded in 1841 by the father of the present proprietor, the latter succeeding to the control about 1869. Mr. H. M. Dearden has had a lengthy experience in all branches of the trade, and is consequently in a position to guarantee the very best class of skilled workmanship in every department. His premises are suitably adapted to the requirements of an important firm and comprise a spacious double-fronted shop, with two floors above, all of which are devoted to business purposes. Great care has been exercised in the fitting as regards machinery, &c., no expense having been spared to equip them thoroughly in this respect. There are several machines, both large and small, the production of the most renowned engineering houses in the kingdom. Mr. Dearden employs a numerous staff, the hands being carefully selected from among highly skilled and experienced artisans. The operations of the firm include all branches incidental to letterpress and copperplate printing, lithography, bookbinding, &c., while among the accessory departments are engraving, stamping, and others of a similar character. The greater part of the work is probably that done for the commercial world and therefore account-book manufacturing forms a highly important feature in which considerable renown has been acquired. A very thriving business is carried on in the general stationery trade, and there is always a large stock of goods. The proprietor also acts as newsagent and bookseller, supplying all the leading London and local newspapers, periodicals, &c., and having a first-class connection among the principal families in this direction. The business throughout is conducted with great ability and enterprise, and to this fact owes its undoubted prominence. Before closing this necessarily somewhat brief notice, it may be mentioned that Mr. Dearden is exceptionally clever as an amateur photographer, and his skill in this respect is clearly evidenced in the various specimens of his work he exhibits, these being mostly photos of places of interest in the locality. They command a large sale, and their artistic merit entitles them to rank among the best productions of this kind to be met with. Mr. Dearden is also registrar of births and deaths in the district, and is widely known both in connection with his business and apart from it for his energy and sound commercial principles

W. S. Barlow, Steam Printer, Stationer, and Account Book Manufacturer, Caxton Works, 7, Fleet Street, Bury.—The important and thoroughly representative business carried on at the above address by Mr. W. S. Barlow was founded by the present proprietor in Haymarket Street, Bury, in the year 1860, and has become one of the leading concerns in the printing and stationery trades in this part of Lancashire. In 1882, with a view to meeting the extended requirements of his increasing business, Mr. Barlow erected the Caxton Works, in Fleet Street, where all his industrial operations are now centralized. These fine premises, which are freehold, stand upon the site formerly occupied by the Old Red Lion, a hotel which in its day was, perhaps, more intimately associated with the past history of Bury than any other within the limits of the borough. In the year 1877 that ancient hostelry and other adjoining properties were purchased by the Corporation, at a cost of £27,000, for purposes of street improvements, the land on which they

stood being then a portion of the glebe. At that time the street at this point was not more than twenty-five feet wide; its present width is about twenty-five yards. Mr. Barlow's new premises eventually rose upon this site, and they now constitute one of the recognized structural ornaments of Bury. They contain five storeys, rising to a total height of 70 feet, and are built in semi-embattled style from designs by Mr. E. Simpkin, of Bury. From their commanding position fine far-reaching views are afforded of the picturesque Irwell valley, extending from Manchester in the south to Bacup in the north. From a practical point of view the Caxton Works satisfy every requirement intended to be met by their erection. They are equipped in all departments with the most improved modern machinery, and the plant has one very notable feature in its principal printing machine, which is one of the largest of its kind yet built, and has a capacity for printing a sheet of paper measuring as much as 70 by 80 inches. The work carried on in the premises, and in which a large and efficient staff is employed, comprises letterpress, lithographic, and copperplate printing, publishing, machine ruling, bookbinding and the manufacture of account-books; also, on the ground floor, a large and attractive shop for the sale of every kind of commercial and fancy stationery. In all these departments Mr. W. S. Barlow has achieved eminent success; and his work has won and maintained a reputation which renders any advertisement of its merits superfluous. The business is directed by the proprietor in person with admirable energy, enterprise and judgment, and as a thoroughly practical and skilful exponent of the several branches of trade and art-industry in which he engages, Mr. Barlow has secured the full confidence and favour of a connection perfectly consistent in value and influence with the first-class character of his business.

Wilson & Ingham, California Mills, Bury.—This business was founded in 1851 by Messrs. Jonathan Wilson and John and Henry Ingham. Mr. Jonathan Wilson died in the year 1873, when the business was continued by Messrs. John and Henry Ingham. In 1882 Mr. John Ingham was removed by death, and since that date the business has been conducted by Mr. Henry and the executors of Mr. John Ingham. This enterprise was commenced with a complement of a hundred looms, in one of the sheds of the present mill. After a period of about four years, however, the rapid development of the concern necessitated increased accommodation, and the firm acquired an adjoining shed, with one hundred and forty looms. About the year 1860 another addition was made to the block of premises by the acquisition of a weaving shed, which had previously been in the occupation of Messrs. Hutchinson, and which Messrs. Wilson & Ingham purchased from the creditors of the previous occupants. This created an addition of two hundred and forty looms, making a complement of four hundred and eighty looms in all. At the close of the American War, however, Messrs. Wilson & Ingham took over the foundry previously occupied by Messrs. Cook & Hacking, converted the same into a weaving-shed, and furnished it with two hundred and forty looms, now making an equipment of seven hundred and twenty looms in all. The premises are supplied with a horizontal engine, by Yates, of Blackburn, of four hundred indicated horse-power, and two boilers, measuring thirty by seven feet, by Clegg, of Heywood. The engine was subsequently converted into a "tendem," by Messrs. Buckley & Taylor, of Oldham. The staple industry of the firm is shirtings; and two hundred and seventy hands are employed. The manufactures of Messrs. Wilson & Ingham are "printers," shirtings and home-trade goods. As is known, "printers" are lighter goods, which are not so highly sized, and are made of a texture suitable for the subsequent process of calico printing. As an evidence of the esteem in which the late Mr. John Ingham was held, it may be stated that a handsome tablet has been erected by the work-people to the memory of that gentleman, in the Wesleyan Chapel in Union Street, with which he was connected. This firm affords a brilliant example of what is meant by the term "self-made men," who by energetic industry have raised themselves to their present leading position in Bury.

Perham & Co., Wine Merchants, 12, Market Street, Bury.—These premises have been tenanted for a period of twenty-six years by leading wine firms, and since 1882 Messrs. Perham & Co. have conducted a large and first-class wholesale trade. Messrs. Perham & Co. have a speciality in a class of wine known as "Vinum Eucharisticum," in which a large trade is done in all parts of Great Britain and Ireland. The great feature of this unique natural wine is that, whilst being the simple product of selected grapes, fermentation has been so conducted as to leave no trace whatever of the flavour of alcohol. Its original grape-juice character is fully retained. It is this distinctive feature of the wine which has established its claim to be used in preference to any other, especially by those of the clergy who require a wine that is entirely free from any admixture of spirit. Professor Estcourt's analysis certifies Vinum Eucharisticum to be "a pure natural wine, and specially fitted for the sacred purpose for which it is intended." The widespread popularity enjoyed by this wine has been won entirely by its own inherent excellence as a genuine unfortified wine. The general wine list of Messrs. Perham & Co. includes—in natural sherries, Palomino, Flor Fino, and Vino de Pasto; in ports, the choicest vintages from 1851, 1858, and 1863 downwards; and also a unique speciality, "Anti-Gout Port," as recommended by leading London physicians; Madeira, from 1820 vintage; clarets, in the best brands and vintages; champagnes, the finest cuvées and vintages of Messrs. Pol Roger & Co.'s celebrated brand, and Charles Gerard's selected cuvée. The spirit list includes very choice liqueur brandy of twenty-four years of age; Irish whiskies of the finest quality; and Scotch whiskies of great age, notably the "Oldbuck," which for mellowness of flavour and high quality stands first amongst the finest productions of the Highland distilleries. Messrs. Perham & Co.'s premises are built in stone, and comprise the ground floor and basement in Market Street, with large and commodious cellars and stores in Market Place and William Street, containing together a large stock in wines and spirits of almost every vintage known to the trade. The firm are gentlemen of enterprise and intelligence, and the entire concern is conducted in a manner befitting its importance.

William Roberts, Tailor and Woollen Draper, Corporation House, 11, Water Street, Bury.—"Corporation House," the name by which the establishment of Mr. W. Roberts is familiarly known, derives its designation from the circumstance that there most of the municipal liveries of the borough are made up. The building is a very handsome one, and has an imposing appearance with the fine spacious plate-glass front on the ground floor, surmounted by ornate architecture, and circular topped double windows, a high-pitched roof, with flag-staff crowning the whole. The building is of brick, four storeys in height, with a 24-feet frontage. The show room is in the basement, and is used solely for the display of ladies' tailor-made garments. At the rear of the shop is the well-appointed office. In another building known as "The Hermitage," there are three work rooms, where well-skilled hands and sewing machines make up the ladies' ulsters, dolmans, silk and cloth jackets, mantles, &c., and other articles of female attire which have now passed out of the rôle of the dressmaker and established themselves in the tailor's workshop. Mr. Roberts founded the business in 1874. He aims only at better-class trade and both as woollen draper and tailor makes no profession of surprising cheapness of articles, in the very limited sense of lowness in price; but he does claim to supply first-class goods at strictly moderate prices; to furnish good material, the best workmanship, and a perfect fit at a fair reasonable figure; and to provide something that will prove absolutely the cheapest and most profitable in the long run, though as to first cost it cannot and has no pretence to compare with slop goods produced in sweating slums. The public of Bury generally who are in a position to acquire good clothing are quite alive to Mr. Roberts's merits as a sartorial provider, and he holds a splendid connection. His stock includes the best goods from the English and Scotch manufacturing districts, most stylish fabrics in all shades and patterns, and in his cutting rooms he is always abreast of the very latest fashions. A department to which special attention is paid is the making of liveries, in which a most extensive trade is done, Mr. Roberts supplying nearly all the leading families in the neighbourhood. For this purpose he has special materials expressly manufactured, which are absolutely waterproof and of the finest possible quality. Mr. Roberts is also an extensive dealer in sewing machines as agent for those of the improved manufacture by Frister & Rossman, Singer, and Wheeler & Wilson makes. One of these Singers made with improvements by Messrs. Frister & Rossman commands a very large sale. There is also an improved Wheeler & Wilson fitted with several most useful patent attachments. Every machine sent out from Mr. Roberts's establishment has the ægis of his personal guarantee which is all important to the buyer whether experienced or otherwise in judgment or marking of the article. Mr. Roberts's business has all round made steady progress from good to better since the commencement and in its daily increasing activity, there are sure signs that it is not yet at its best.

Jackson Brothers, Seed Merchants, Millers, and Sizing Flour Manufacturers, Knowsley Corn Mills, Bury.—This business was founded in or about the year 1839; the present premises were opened by Messrs. Jackson Brothers, who are still the proprietors, and who have won a high reputation in the trade for the excellence of their products. Knowsley Corn Mills occupy a large area of ground and consist of a fine stone building of three storeys in height, with spacious warehouses and a handsome office. The mills proper are equipped in first-rate style with all the most approved appliances and machinery required for the important work carried on, the machinery being driven by a powerful steam-engine by Whitaker, of Accrington, the boiler being one of Lord's, of Bury. Amongst other products that of sizing flour forms the speciality of the firm, and on account of its suitableness for the calico printing and cotton manufacturing industry it is in great demand, keeping Knowsley Mills constantly busy. The trade of the firm in the seed department is chiefly with agriculturists, who look upon this house's products as being the most prolific in the market. Consequently an extensive business is done in the farming districts of Lancashire. Messrs. Jackson Brothers number amongst their supporters the most influential calico printers, bleachers and finishers in England, and their specialities and the honourable methods that have always characterised the management of their business continue to maintain and extend the old-established reputation of the firm.

Samuel Smith, Clothier, Mantle Maker and General Warehouseman, 15 and 17, King Street, Bury.—This old-established business was commenced in 1812 by the grandfather of the present proprietor, in premises at the top of King Street, and at that time was confined to the woollen drapery. On the demise of the founder, and in consequence of the rapid development of the business and the necessity for increased accommodation, Mr. Smith, senior, built the present extensive premises at 15 and 17, King Street, which were also used for manufacturing many of the woollens that had gained such repute. These premises again, in time, became too small to keep pace with an ever-widening trade, and the weaving, &c., had to be sent elsewhere to make room for the variety of stocks necessary to be held as department after department was added. There is no outside show or ostentation connected with this establishment, such adventitious aids to celebrity being altogether ignored, the firm relying solely on the sterling quality of their goods. The extensive workroom accommodation, with every improved appliance, affords unusual facilities for the effective and economical working of a large and increasing business. The stock is very large and comprehensive, being replete with all the best features of the various lines engaged in, and thoroughly representative of the trade in all those branches, embracing, as it does, a large assortment of iron and brass bedsteads, bedding, and bed furniture, Brussels, Kidderminster, and Wilton carpets, rugs, &c.; in addition to the heavy stocks of woollens specially manufactured for the firm, and the season's requirements in general drapery. Pianos also form a leading feature with this firm. The present Mr. Smith has had a long connection with the leading English manufacturers, whose instruments he has supplied for many years with the greatest satisfaction. In the general clothing and mantle department the firm is well employed, supplying both the trade and private customers. All goods of this class are made to order by specially qualified and experienced workpeople, and of the very best materials and of guaranteed workmanship. The business in every department receives the strict personal attention of the proprietor, and is conducted throughout with marked ability, energy, and enterprise. A staff of travellers is sent out continually, and the trade controlled is of a widespread, influential, and steadily-growing character. Mr. Samuel Smith, who is now the sole proprietor, occupies a prominent and influential position in mercantile circles, and the family is well known and highly esteemed for their long and honourable connection with Bury, and also for their active exertions in promoting the best interests of the commerce and industries of the town and district.

William Bailey, Wholesale and Retail Glass, China, and Earthenware Merchant, 20, Haymarket Street, Bury.—The staple branch of British commerce comprised in the glass, China, and earthenware trade is appropriately represented by the centrally situated depot conducted by Mr. William Bailey, the founder and sole proprietor, the business having been established by him upwards of thirty years ago, and the present premises opened in 1880. The spacious window of the mart is well fitted with a large and varied assortment of general goods: breakfast, dinner, and tea services being the most prominent, and a glimpse at the interior reveals a large and comprehensive stock of the best and finest quality. There is every possible article incidental to the trade on hand, though it is easy to perceive that the specialities are the breakfast, dinner, and tea services before referred to, which it is worthy of note, are of exceptionally good manufacture, unique in design, and richly ornamented in brilliant colours, while there are those of a subdued shade suited to the taste of the more æsthetic, but the highest and humblest classes will find the very article suited to their requirements in this specially well-selected stock. In glass goods, the tumblers, decanters, wine-glasses, dessert dishes, &c., are all of superior make and well worth inspection by those about to furnish or wish to replenish their stock. Another speciality consists of glass globes, an immense variety being kept on hand in all the most approved shapes. They can be had in stout or thin glass and with or without stands, the superior manufacture of the glass rendering the globes beautifully clear and transparent, and well worth the attention of antiquaries, horticulturists, scientists, and others for the preservation of specimens of all kinds, the protection of artificial flowers, groups of birds, &c. Then again, gardeners' pots are kept on hand in great variety, made of the best ironstone clay, and finished in a superior manner for all kinds of bedding-out plants and other horticultural purposes. There is a room at the rear of the premises well stocked and devoted exclusively to the wholesale department, in which an immense business is done with small shopkeepers and hawkers who visit the surrounding villages. Publicans are also supplied with all kinds of measured pint and gill pots, also jugs of every design. The general trade is very extensive and well established. Mr. Bailey is a gentleman of great experience in this line of commerce, and highly esteemed by all with whom he has business transactions.

Clayton Brothers, General Drapers and Silk Mercers and Furriers, 60, Fleet Street, Bury.—This business was established in 1886 by Messrs. Clayton who are still the sole proprietors and who have made it one of the most popular of the kind in Bury. The premises are of large extent, and situated in a prominent position in Fleet Street, with most tastefully arranged windows which have a very attractive appearance. Handsomely fitted up and admirably arranged the establishment displays to advantage a magnificent stock of general and fancy drapery, gloves, ribbons, corsets, and ladies' outfitting generally. In the black and coloured dress department they have always on view one of the largest assortments in the district, and have secured for themselves a distinct reputation in this department of their business. In the dressmaking departments an efficient staff of hands is employed, and on account of the reputation enjoyed by the firm for the excellence of style, fit, and workmanship in the dresses they turn out, Messrs. Clayton Brothers do an extensive and influential business in this important department. In furs, silks, and general drapery they also do a flourishing trade, while in the glove department it is an open secret that their turn-out is immense. It may be interesting to point out that Messrs. Clayton Brothers have required on several occasions to enlarge and rearrange their premises at 60, Fleet Street, owing to the flattering measure of success which has attended their business efforts, and that their latest enterprise has been to thoroughly rebuild their shop front, adding eighty square feet of plate glass to their already large accommodation, in order to still further extend and improve those window displays for which they enjoy so enviable a reputation. Messrs. Clayton are agreeable, courteous gentlemen well known in the trade, and they are much respected by their numerous warm supporters for the efforts they have made to supply the finest and most durable class of goods at prices which compete most successfully with all the trade.

[Since the body of the above notice was put into type we regret to add that the death of Mr. E. A. Clayton has taken place. In consequence of this Clayton Brothers have given up the shop, 21, Rock Street, and have transferred the whole of their business to the old address, 60, Fleet Street, as described above.]

Joseph Sykes & Sons, Lower Mill, Bury.—To Messrs. Joseph Sykes & Sons, of the Lower Mill, Bury, Lancashire, belongs the unique position of being the only manufacturers of braids, window cords, crinoline steels, laces, &c., in this district. The mill of the firm consists of two sheds and warehouse of two floors, the whole covering an area of about two thousand five hundred square yards. The sheds contain a large number of cord and braid plaiting machines, and altogether, a complement of seventy-five thousand spindles are at work here. There are two engines, one being constructed on the vertical and the other on the horizontal principle, built by Bland, of Bury. There is also a substantial boiler, thirty feet by seven feet, by Joseph Lord, of the same town. Mr. Joseph Sykes, who founded the concern in 1844, has been dead some years and the business has since been carried on by four of his sons. Mr. William Sykes, one of the partners, has for some years past, represented with much acceptance the Moorside ward (in which these works are situated) in the Town Council of Bury. The firm have a very wide business connection, and occupy a warehouse in London, and similar premises in Manchester. The partners are pushing and enterprising men of business attainments and sound practical qualifications, and are conducting this important manufacturing concern with the most gratifying success.

Hutchinson Bros., Victoria Boiler Works, Bury.—Founded in the year 1870 by J. Hutchinson & Son, this business was acquired by the present proprietors, Messrs. Hutchinson Bros., in 1884. The premises are of large extent, consisting of spacious yards, boiler works, and offices. Equipped in first-class style, with all the most approved modern machinery for planing plates, boring, instead of punching, and riveting, the Victoria Boiler Works are constantly engaged in the construction of Cornish, portable, vertical, and other boilers of iron and steel, and for low and high pressures. This house is also famous all over England, and in many foreign countries, for bleaching and other keirs, jacketed pans, tanks, girders, and other work in wrought iron and steel. The trade of the firm extends all over Great Britain and Ireland, and their Cornish and vertical boilers especially reach foreign ports in large numbers. Messrs. Hutchinson enjoy a high reputation for their thorough practical knowledge of boiler construction, and their opinion as to the efficiency of old boilers is highly valued. Consequently they do an extensive business in making alterations and repairs for clients in and around Lancashire, which work is done in all cases under their careful personal supervision. Messrs. Hutchinson are agreeable, courteous gentlemen, whose honourable methods in the management of their business and promptitude in meeting urgent demands have won for them a high place in the esteem and confidence of the most influential firms in these parts.

Richard Millett, Cotton and Cotton-waste Merchant, Bury Bridge and Knowsley Street, Bury.—The offices and principal warehouses of the firm are situated in Knowsley Street, and occupy a handsome building of three floors and basement, constructed of grey Yorkshire stone. This establishment forms the headquarters of the firm, and has a handsome suite of offices, with private room for the principal. The bulk of the stock is kept at Duke Street Mill, and the chief waste stores are situated at Wyke's Woollen Mills, at corner of Duke Street and Knowsley Street. This is an extensive establishment, measuring 150 feet in Duke Street and 75 feet in Knowsley Street, and being four storeys in height. The premises are equipped in first-rate style with hydraulic presses for baling and machines for willowing the waste, a powerful condensing engine being used to drive these. This extensive establishment is used exclusively for the preparation and storage of waste, Mr. Millett being one of the largest dealers in Lancashire. The trade of the firm extends all over Lancashire and the cotton districts of Yorkshire, and requires ten horses and lurries, which are constantly employed in conveying goods to and from the railway stations. Mr. Millett is a well-known gentleman, and enjoys the esteem of all with whom he comes in contact, whether in connection with business or matters affecting the public interest.

Sedgwick & Heap, Merchants and Manufacturers, Rock Street and Eden Street, Bury; Warehouse, 23, High Street, Manchester. This firm was established in Stanley Street in a small shop in the year 1871; they were bought out by the Corporation; they then built the present extensive premises, and came into occupation in 1885. These latter comprise a building of three storeys with a handsome double frontage. The principal window in Rock Street and Eden Street is dressed most artistically with a splendid assortment of goods in general drapery, silk dress pieces, and mantles, and occupies a very conspicuous position, presenting a very elegant appearance, and forming a centre of much attraction. The window in Rock Street is also well dressed with a good selection of West of England suiting, Scotch and Irish tweeds, &c.; also with a large and choice assortment of men's and boys' ready-made clothing, which is made on their extensive premises by experienced hands. They also display a large assortment of carpets in Brussels, Axminster, Kidderminster, tapestry, &c., linoleums, floorcloths, mats, and rugs in endless variety, together with brass and iron bedsteads, &c. They have extensive rooms for carpet-planning, and are open to take furnishing contracts to any extent, their reputation in this particular branch being both widespread and thoroughly deserved. The goods are of the most satisfactory character, the styles excellent, and the finish of material all that could be desired, and ladies, gentlemen, and juveniles alike can be suited most thoroughly with all that pertains to matters of dress. Messrs. Sedgwick & Heap have also wholesale warehouse premises at No. 23, High Street, Manchester. This is a business managed in all its details with consummate skill and the most strict attention, the partners being gentlemen of much experience and indisputable taste. An adequate staff of assistants are engaged, and among the prosperous business houses of the locality that of Messrs. Sedgwick & Heap occupies a very conspicuous position.

F. Rothwell, Maker of Shuttles, Picking Sticks, Beam Wedges, &c., Mason Street, Bury.—Founded in the year 1870 by Messrs. James Rothwell and his sons, Henry and Francis, this business is now the property of Mr. Francis, the senior member having died in 1884 and Mr. Henry having retired from the concern in 1877. The works are equipped in first-rate style with all the most approved machinery for wood-working, and several special appliances belonging to the manufacture of shuttles, picking sticks, beam wedges, and other articles required in weaving mills, the machinery being driven by a powerful steam-engine by Walmsley, of Bury. The trade of the firm is very extensive, a large business being done with continental firms of the most influential order, and with the principal manufacturers in England and Scotland. Using only the highest quality of thoroughly seasoned woods in their manufactures, and Mr. Rothwell's reputed powers of adaptation and mechanical skill are among the secrets by which this house enjoys its prominent position in this important trade. Mr. Rothwell is well known in Bury, and on account of his agreeable courteous manner and upright principles he is much respected by all with whom he comes in contact.

Robert Battersby & Sons, Woollen Merchants, 7, Parson's Lane, Bury.—This business was established in 1810 by the grandfather of the present head of the firm. Mr. Robert Battersby, his son, died some years ago, and the surviving partner is Mr. John Battersby, the son of the late Mr. Richard Battersby. The premises have a business-like appearance, and a good sound trade is transacted on lines which have known probably no change in method since the firm was established. Their chief trade is in blankets, flannels, shirts, counterpanes, and woollen goods generally. The blankets and flannels form a speciality, the firm being celebrated for these goods, which no other house in the trade can place in the market on better terms. The premises are commodious, without any effort being made at show or pretension. There is a large packing warehouse fitted up with hand press, as also offices, and four storeys devoted to storage purposes, the frontage of the establishment extending to upwards of forty feet. The trade conducted by Messrs. Robert Battersby & Sons is chiefly confined to Manchester and Liverpool, and other Lancashire towns, only a home business being effected. This is a concern ably conducted and highly and deservedly appreciated by a large and important connection.

Thomas Cornall, Plumber and Ironmonger, &c., Haymarket Street, and Commercial Buildings, Bury.—This business has been in existence just over forty years. The premises comprise a spacious three-storeyed building of which one portion constitutes a showroom, in which is kept a very extensive assortment of all descriptions of material, &c., used in the various branches of industry comprised within the scope of

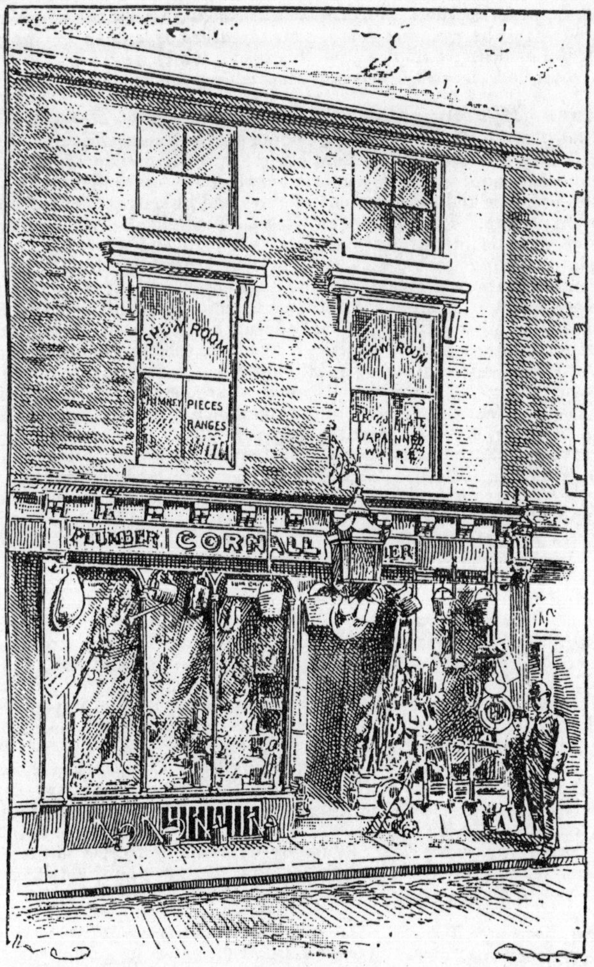

the firm's operations. There are several large storerooms in which is a very extensive supply of all kinds of goods, fittings, general material, &c., into the details of which it would be impracticable to enter. The firm have spacious works in Commercial Buildings, Spring Street, where a large number of hands are employed. At the commencement of 1889,

WORKS, COMMERCIAL BUILDINGS,
SPRING STREET

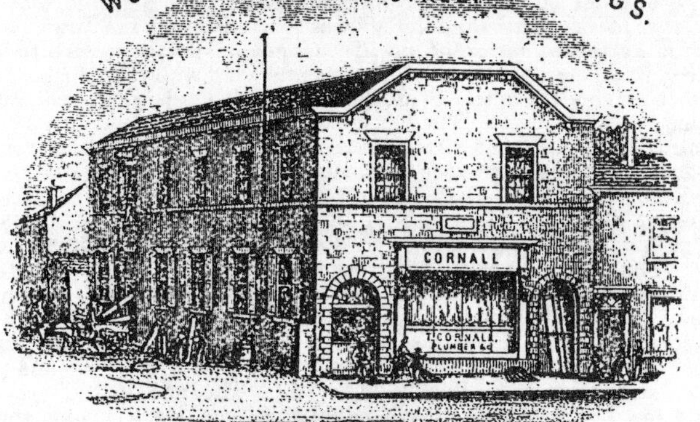

Mr. Cornall opened a general and furnishing ironmongery department at 8, Haymarket Street, with a stock specially selected to meet modern requirements. This branch of the business is under the management of his son, T. H. Cornall, whose experience in one of the principal ironmongery establishments in Manchester is of the utmost value in this connection. The stock of this branch includes a splendid collection of kitchen requisites, ranges, kitcheners, and cooking ranges of the latest improved designs. In connection with this department the setting up and fixing are confided to none but skilled workmen, thus avoiding the inevitable complaints and annoyances arising from ranges being badly fitted up. In chimney-pieces and grates Mr. Cornall is sole agent for the Abbotsford slow combustion grate, &c., and those who contemplate building or making alterations will find it to their advantage to inspect his stock of chimney-pieces and register grates, which for newness of design cannot be surpassed, and will be found to comprise all varieties of marble. There is also an excellent assortment of brass goods; the stock of brass kerbs, fire brasses, rests, coal vases, fire screens, sconces, gongs, letter racks, &c., comprising all the newest designs. In addition Mr. Cornall is agent for the Leeds atmospheric door check and spring, which is a most successful invention. The business is ably conducted, and Mr. Cornall is well known, not only commercially, but as a magistrate of the borough, in which position he has displayed great ability. His establishment is highly popular in the trade and commands a large connection in all parts of the district.

Wilson & Stockall, Carriage Builders, &c., Henry Street, Union Square; Central Show Rooms, Castle Buildings, Market Place (opposite Sir Robert Peel's statue), Bury.—This firm was established in the year 1877, their works occupying the basement and three storeys and workshops in Henry Street, in addition to which they have extensive warehouse and timber stores in Back King Street. There is also a large yard and excellent accommodation for their customers' repairs, &c. They have special machinery of their own for bending and the instantaneous cooling of wheel tyres. The chief speciality of Messrs. Wilson & Stockall is what is known as their "Medical Gig," which is recognised as peculiarly adapted for the use of medical men, being light in construction, and yet capable of hard wear. They also make a light and graceful vehicle, called a "Canoe Landau," as also a "Double Brougham," which has acquired much reputation, also an "Ambulance Brougham," made for hospital purposes, several of which have been supplied to various corporate and governing bodies. This firm maintain a very high position as builders of carriages. They are thoroughly practical men, and have succeeded admirably in securing lightness of draught and comfort in riding by constructing all their carriages on true mechanical principles, and with carefully selected materials under their own personal superintendence. Messrs. Wilson & Stockall are holders of prize certificates from several agricultural and other county shows and exhibitions, also gold medallists for superior manufacture of carriages, &c. They have just introduced a special steel tyre which is so constructed as to keep the wheels of any vehicle out of the tram lines. The firm has recently opened a handsome suite of show rooms in Castle Buildings, where a choice collection of their most noted manufactures is on exhibition and presents a very attractive appearance in this popular thoroughfare. Repairs of every description are executed with the most strict promptitude, and estimates and designs cheerfully forwarded. Messrs. Wilson & Stockall have been recipients of the patronage of the leading ladies and gentlemen of the district. Their works are in a most prosperous condition, and there are certainly none who know the men but will feel gratified by their success.

Webster & Peacock, Grocers and Italian Warehousemen, 5, Silver Street, Bury.—This business has been carried on for well nigh a hundred years in the same premises. At the beginning of the present century the building was known all over the town and neighbourhood as the "Old Black Boy." How it came to be so designated is not positively known. Certain it is it was once a celebrated tobacconist's establishment, and many such bore the name of the "Old Black Boy." Be this as it may, the "Old Black Boy" of Bury was converted into a grocery store by a Mr. Moscrop who occupied the premises for fifty years. He was succeeded by Mr. Heyes who continued the business till his death in 1873, when the present proprietors took it over. Messrs. Webster and Peacock's shop is one of the handsomest in the trade to be seen in Bury or within a radius of many miles of its boundaries. It has a frontage of twenty-four feet, and one of the most attractively dressed windows to be seen anywhere, presenting a splendid and beautifully arranged display of all the highest classes of goods comprised in the stock of Italian warehousemen of the first order. The business is one of the best in the borough, and some idea of its importance may be formed from the fact that twelve assistants are employed and their horses and vans are always busily engaged delivering goods to customers. The concern has not merely an ancient record but also a very high reputation for the general excellence of the wares vended at it. No man can well be a half century in any business which undertakes the supply of articles of daily requirement, and the quality of which can be pronounced upon by every consumer when they reach his table, unless it is well and widely known that the goods can be thoroughly depended on, and the present proprietors are most careful to maintain and improve upon the old good name of their emporium. The firm are also agents for Messrs. W. & A. Gilbey's wines and spirits, and they have constantly on hand a large and varied stock of goods of that world-renowned house.

R. Jackson's Boot and Shoe Warehouse, 25, Fleet Street, Bury.—This business was founded in 1872, and from the very commencement has increased and developed in a very rapid degree, and in order to meet the requirements of a very extensive trade, the proprietor has lately opened a branch establishment at 29, Princess Street. The establishment in Fleet Street consists of a large shop having a commanding frontage of over forty feet, and being heavily stocked with a choice assortment of superior boots and shoes. In the rear of the showroom there is a ladies' room for measuring and fitting purposes, and the whole of the arrangements are upon the very best scale. Mr. Jackson keeps a very large stock and undertakes to supply the wants of all classes so far as boots and shoes are concerned; as he himself puts the matter in a somewhat novel form of handbill, there are "boots for every kind of station, boots for every occupation; boots for wholesale, boots for retail, boots in many styles of detail." All goods are of a very superior quality, durability of the workmanship and material being points to which the proprietor's attention is particularly directed. Some classes of boots are intended for hard and rough wear, and are made with extra regard to durability, while in others elegance is duly studied, and a pair of boots can be produced unsurpassed for style, fit, and economy by any house in the trade, and sold at a price that will compare very favourably with those charged in any part of the kingdom. A large trade is done among all sections of the public with whom the establishment has attained a remarkable degree of popularity. Repairing is a department in which the firm are extensively engaged, an adequate staff of experienced hands being employed upon the premises. All orders are carried out upon the most approved principles and with commendable promptitude and punctuality. The business is in fact admirably conducted in every respect, and the great success which has been achieved by the energy and enterprise of the proprietor is undoubtedly well merited.

A. Ashworth & Son, Hat Merchants and Manufacturers, 3, Silver Street, and Fernhill, Bury, and Hooley Hill, Manchester. —Mr. Adam Ashworth was the pioneer of the hat manufacturing industry in Bury, with which pursuit the Ashworth family have been connected for a period of more than one hundred and twenty-five years. In 1858 Mr. John Ashworth, the founder of the concern, died at the age of 86, having been nearly all his life engaged in the business, having laid the foundation of a business which has since developed into a most important concern. The name of this gentleman will be long cherished throughout the county in connection with the Wesleyan Methodist movement. He was the principal stay and leading supporter of Methodism in this locality at its commencement, and was the intimate friend of John Wesley. His son, Mr. Adam Ashworth, the head of the existing firm, has been instrumental in developing the business to its present large wholesale proportions. The firm have extensive works at Fernhill, Bury, Hooley Hill, and Guide Bridge, near Manchester. The firm at Fernhill is known as A. Ashworth & Sons; that at Hooley Hill as Adam Ashworth, Junr., while the Silver Street establishment is conducted under the title of A. & A. Ashworth. A very large staff of hands are employed by the firm at their various establishments. The shop, in style, is one of the very best in Bury, and has a frontage of thirty feet. Only the very highest class of trade is carried on here. Mr. Abel Ashworth has the personal superintendence of this branch, and is aided by a staff of experienced assi tants. The business is conducted in a manner befitting its long prestige and established reputation, and enjoys that success to which hard persevering work and steady effort have justly entitled it.

E. Redfern, Draper, &c., Silver Street, Bury.—The extensive and important business concern conducted by Mr. E. Redfern, as a draper, hosier, glover, and outfitter, at Silver Street, Bury, occupies a large brick building of three stories in height, and containing a frontage of sixty feet in Silver Street, the most central district in the town of Bury. Many years ago there stood on this site a highly popular and celebrated hotel known as The Eagle and Child, which before the era of railway enterprise served as the principal posting-house of Bury. On their occupation by Mr. E. Redfern, the premises were subjected to a very material alteration, a large proportion being entirely rebuilt and the whole converted into the present handsome bazaar-like warehouse, in which an extensive trade in general drapery, toy, and fancy goods is carried on. The shop is seventy-five feet in length, by twenty-five feet wide. At all times an attractive establishment (and made so by reason of the cheapness of the commodities sold here), it is at Christmastide and the new year that "Redfern's" can be seen to the greatest advantage. At that festive season this emporium is truly a scene of busy activity, converted for the time being into a German fair, decorated in all the hues of colour which artistic taste can suggest, and brilliantly lighted by lanterns of delicate shading and material. Thousands of visitors (largely composed of the juvenile community of the district) are to be met with making Christmas purchases in the various departments. This is the only establishment in Bury where the new American cash railway is in use; an invention which greatly facilitates the conveyance of change to and from customers. There are two immense plate-glass windows, through which are displayed a vast assortment of drapery and fancy goods. One room of fifteen feet in length, at the end of the front premises, serves as heavy goods warehouse, and is approached by descending two steps. Here there is kept a large stock of blankets, rugs, carpets, sheeting, quilts, &c. There is a handsome balcony around the premises, entirely devoted to ladies' and children's outfitting, costumes, mantles, mackintoshes, &c. The large cellars are used as packing and unpacking departments. There are five large stock rooms on its second floor, and five rooms of equal dimensions on the third floor, from which the sale shop is replenished. Sixteen assistants are regularly employed; but at Christmastide when the German fancy fair is in operation, the staff is very largely augmented. The hosiery department is well stocked with every variety of goods known to. this trade. The millinery section is carried on in an apartment on the first floor. Here is a splendid display of hats, bonnets, feathers, ribbons, and artificial flowers, the whole being arranged with the greatest taste. Mr. Redfern is a man of the most thorough business principles, and his trade, which is conducted on the cash system, is in a most deservedly flourishing condition.

James Byrom, Joiner, Builder, and Brickmaker, Woolfold, Bury.—This extensive business presents many features of more than ordinary interest. Mr. Byrom commenced business in 1868, and has been probably more intimately associated than any other man in his line with the progress and development of Bury and its neighbourhood for the last twenty years. In Whitelegge Street, Woolfold, Mr. Byrom has an extensive establishment, comprising timber-yard and saw-mills, joiners' shops, lath-rending works, &c. The various departments are replete with powerful and improved machinery and appliances, including circular and band saws, also moulding and morticing machines, tenoning and rebating machines, and other appliances, embodying all the latest improvements and the most comprehensive utilities. The brickyard is situated at Brown Hill, Tottington, and is of considerable extent, and equipped with machinery and steam power. The firm have likewise a large stone quarry at Wrigley Close, Tottington, in Bury, the stone from which is admirably adapted for paving, building, and monumental purposes. The business in every department receives the strict personal attention of the proprietor, and is conducted throughout with marked ability, energy, and enterprise. It is also satisfactory to note that in spite of the prevailing depression in these industries, that Mr. Byrom is well employed in every branch of his business; and so complete are all the arrangements of the works, and the large amount of improved machinery at command, together with the number of skilled and experienced workmen regularly employed, that the firm stand in an unrivalled position to undertake and execute contracts and work of any magnitude, at the shortest notice and with dispatch and economy. The following is a list of recent contracts, either completed or in hand:—£16,000, Broughton Bridge Paper Mills, sole contract; £60,000, Lancashire and Yorkshire Railway canal contracts; £2,000, Lancashire and Yorkshire Railway bridges, &c., Bolton; £5,000, Olive Paper Works, Woolfold; £6,000, Crompton's Paper Works, Elton; £2,000, Ramsbottom Paper Mills; £6,000, British section Brussels Exhibition; £11,000, Wood Pulp Works, Goole; £1,100, bakery, &c., Bury Co-operative Society; £38,000, thirty-eight villa residences, Old Trafford, Manchester; £5,000, extensions to Children's Home, Edgworth; £15,000, gas retort house, gas purifying house, gas meter house, destructor house, alterations to offices, Bury Corporation work. Mr. James Byrom has a first-class business connection extending to all parts of the county, of Bury and the district, and is well known and highly esteemed in mercantile circles.

The Derby Hotel, Bury, Lancashire, Mr. William Clark, Proprietor.—The family of the "Lords of Knowsley" has for centuries held property in this ancient and historic town, and in 1850 the late Earl of Derby built the hotel under notice, from designs by the celebrated Sir H. Smirk. Its first occupant was a Mr. Chorlton; two years afterwards it came into possession of the Handley family of the celebrated old house, the "Eagle and Child," in Silver Street, and passed from father to son until the year 1880, when it was acquired by the present proprietor, Mr. William Clark, who had previously great experience in this line as the manager of the Palace and Prince of Wales's Hotels at Southport. The Derby Hotel is a handsome stone structure of fine proportions and noble architectural appearance, with a frontage of fully 135 feet to Market Street and the Market Place, and with the Town Hall, to which it is attached, forms the most prominent and attractive feature of this locality. Attached to the hotel is a spacious yard with stabling for fifteen horses, coach houses, lofts, and all the accessories of a large and thoroughly organised establishment. The house contains coffee and commercial rooms, dining room, three large sitting rooms, kitchens, and the usual domestic offices, together with upwards of twenty lofty and comfortable bed-rooms. The dining room is an apartment of handsome proportions, and it is interesting to note that when H.R.H. Prince Albert Victor visited Bury in 1888, a luncheon was given here in his honour, at which 150 guests sat down. The hotel throughout is furnished and fitted in a very superior style, and an air of comfort and luxury pervades the whole house. The cuisine is under the direction of an experienced "chef," whose efforts are highly appreciated by the numerous patrons. The cellars are well stocked with wines and spirits of the best brands, and with ale, beer and porter from the London and Burton breweries. The principal Freemasons' lodges are held here, viz., one Craft Lodge, one Mark Lodge, and one Arch Lodge, as well as the Mayor's dinners and public banquets, luncheons, &c. The hotel is well patronised by both residents and visitors, and is the resort of the gentry of the county and the principal manufacturers and merchants. Both Mr. and Mrs. Clark take an active part in the management, they are well known and highly respected, and by strict attention to the comforts of their guests, spirited enterprise and genial courtesy, they have secured the confidence and support of a very extensive and highly distinguished patronage.

G. Hewart, Silk Mercer and Linen Draper, 9, Fleet Street, Bury.—This business, which is one of the recognised business concerns of the county, was established by the present proprietor in 1867. The premises comprise a large and handsomely appointed building of five storeys in height, containing a frontage of thirty feet. Mr. Hewart is at the present date conducting one of the most popular and successful trades in Bury as a silk mercer and linen draper. This gentleman turns out an annual average of a thousand dresses, employing a staff of forty assistants in the dress and mantle making department of his business alone. The large premises on the basement are repletely stocked with a magnificent range of goods in silks and wool dress fabrics of British and foreign manufacture, and general drapery; a fine display of well-made eiderdown quilts being specially noticeable. The windows

are dressed with most artistic taste, and, from the fine judgment exhibited in the selection and blending of colour, present a very attractive appearance. Upstairs are fourteen rooms, all devoted to the work of this business. It is a just demand on the part of the civilisation of the nineteenth century that matters of dress shall receive a due consideration, and this is a demand which has been and is being complied with to a most gratifying extent. In the establishment of Mr. G. Hewart, of Bury, the large *clientèle* of that gentleman have a superb stock from which to make a selection of goods in every shade and design, and unequalled on the score of value, and in Mr. G. Hewart the ladies of Bury and district have a business man on whose taste and judgment in dress and fashion they can at all times place a most firm reliance.

W. A. Duckworth, Fish, Game, and Poultry Salesman, English and Foreign Fruiterer, 9, Silver Street, Bury.—The extensive business controlled by Mr. W. A. Duckworth, fish, game, and poultry salesman, English and foreign fruiterer, of 9, Silver Street, Bury, is a standing illustration of how great things may be accomplished from

small beginnings by men of industry, energy, and perseverance. Mr. Duckworth is eminently a self-made man in the best sense of the term. He began as a dealer on a small scale in the Bury Market, but owing to his business tact and pushing disposition, soon rose to distinction in his calling, and to the management of larger transactions. He entered on his present premises about fifteen years ago. They are cloce to the Market Place and in one of the best situations in the borough. The shop is a handsome one, double-fronted, and measures thirty-five feet square. It is excellently appointed for the trade, lofty, and well-ventilated, and the marble slabs on which the piscatory wares are placed present quite a refreshing and appetising appearance. He has always a large stock of all kinds of fish in their various seasons in perfectly fresh condition, and goes very extensively into the oyster trade. Then when their time comes there is a fine show of four-footed and winged game, and at no mart is the beginning of the festivals of St. Grouse, St. Partridge, and St. Pheasant more promptly marked by the first fruits of the moors, the stubbles, and preserves, than at the Silver Street Game Emporium; while all the year round he presents the plumpest specimens of the produce of the farmyard, and at Christmastide makes really an immense show of turkeys, geese, ducks, and other favourite contributors to the festive board. But fish, fowl, and game represent only one-half of his business, the other consists in home and foreign fruit in which he has a very high-class trade. Every conceivable article for the proper furnishing of the dessert table is to be found in its season at his mart and always in prime order, for his supplies come forward with the utmost regularity, and anything having the least suspicion of staleness is at once put aside. Mr. Duckworth learnt in his early days that the surest way to success in such a business as his was to vend only what would give the customer entire satisfaction, and he puts that principle in constant practice; while his supply connections are so well organized that he is ever first, and often the only merchant in the field as regards the more costly and particular dainties. Thus early grapes, peaches, and kindred hothouse fruits are often to be found in his shop when they would be sought for in vain elsewhere. His great success is therefore no matter of wonder. He gives diligent personal attention to all branches of his trade, and has a goodly staff of assistants, porters, game-dressers, &c., while he employs two horses, a market cart, and trap exclusively for business purposes. A more flourishing concern of its order is not to be found in Lancashire.

John Catton, General Stay Manufacturer, 5, Fleet Street, Bury.—This flourishing concern was founded by the present owner's father in 1849, and has never been known under any other title. The factory is a large brick structure of four storeys, in which are three spacious workrooms all devoted to purposes of manufacture, the remainder of the edifice being utilised for store-rooms and the conduct of the commercial and financial part of the business. There is an excellent working plant, including several machines by Bradbury, Carver, Seller, &c., specially adapted to this kind of work, by the Singer Manufacturing Company, and two by the well-known firm of Bradbury; and in addition a full staff of experienced operatives are regularly employed. The operations of the house include the production of all kinds of stays and corsets, for which only the best seasoned materials are used, and the most skilled labour employed, and consequently Catton's stays and corsets are always in great demand among the best buying houses in the trade. The great speciality, however, for which the establishment has for many years been noted is "the Lancashire" stay, which is particularly well made and highly recommended for the trim and *svelte* appearance which it imparts to the wearer. The several goods manufactured by the house are largely bought by the drapers of surrounding towns and villages, and, being well known everywhere for their durability, command a ready sale locally at good quotations. The proprietor is a gentleman practically acquainted with every branch of the industry he carries on, and highly respected by his customers for his courtesy and attention to their orders on all occasions.

James Wood, Tailor and Woollen Draper, 22, Market Street, Bury.—This flourishing business was founded some years ago in Princess Street, and has been located at the present address since 1883. The premises comprise a large and well-appointed double-fronted shop, in the spacious window of which are displayed a choice assortment of piece goods, such as Angolas, cheviots, cashmeres, homespuns, meltons, serges, flannels, West of England coatings, vicunas, &c., all of the finest texture and finish, and, in addition, a large reserve stock is always kept on hand to meet any additional demands that may be made upon the house. Mr. Wood confines himself entirely to the best descriptions of work, and as there are no cheap fabrics to be found on the premises, the purchaser may rely on the garments procured at this establishment being in every way first-class, for in addition to quality of material the proprietor secures quality of workmanship both in the cutting, fitting, and making-up departments. About a dozen tailors, all picked workmen, and a first-class cutter are employed regularly. Mr. Wood, too, takes an active part in the general organization of the business. The basis of the high reputation the house has acquired in the town and neighbourhood is unquestionably laid by the fact that the definite object

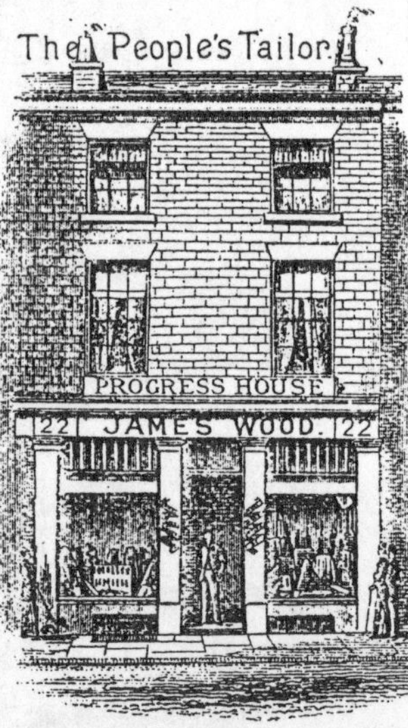

of the proprietor is to produce artistic, well-made clothing of the best materials, and such as will in every respect give entire satisfaction to his numerous *clientèle*, and this he is enabled to do by his long experience and matured judgment in the technics of the trade. The connection is a first-class one, and well established.

Driffield Brothers, Silk Mercers, &c., Bolton Street and Market Place, Bury.—This extensive business was established in 1858. The premises consist of a fine handsome stone building of four storeys in height with a double frontage. The portion of the premises situated in Bolton Street contains two windows, with a most attractive display of silk dress pieces and fancy drapery of every description. Four windows abut on the Market Place, and have a frontage of 70 feet. The windows are devoted to heavy goods, carpets of the Brussels, Axminster, and Kidderminster makes being the most prominent. For the Christmas and New Year holiday season Messrs. Driffield Brothers display a charming assortment of fancy toys of every description, lighted up with Chinese lanterns, forming a German fair—a most pleasing and ingenious exhibition. The sale shop is located on the basement, and measures 120 feet by 80 feet, in which, amongst other valuable goods, are displayed an immense quantity of lace curtains, many of which are of the most exquisite designs and finish. The firm make a speciality of this department. In a large room on the first floor is a splendidly equipped carpet room, with an enormous stock. The mantle and millinery rooms are on the second floor, where a large staff of lady assistants is engaged in these attractive and important departments. This floor also contains a suite of showrooms of perfect construction and arrangement. The trade conducted by Messrs. Driffield Brothers is of the best middle-class ready-money business, but there is in every department one strikingly prominent feature—and that is, the excellent value given by the firm. The order and system are excellent, and the person would be more than ordinarily devoid of observation who failed to detect throughout the entire establishment the unmistakeable evidence of a thoroughly practical administration, governed by all the laws of good taste.

Simeon Dawson, late Bury Carriage Company, Coach Proprietor, Office and Stables, Taylor Street, Bury.—Originally a weaver Mr. Dawson became a greengrocer and kept a hearse and one horse, the hearse being of a type that has long been out of fashion. His premises at this time were situated in Water Street, nearly opposite the Boar's Head Inn. As his business here increased he took a lease of the stables adjoining the Boar's Head which he retained until 1878. In 1873 he purchased an old weaving shed in Taylor Street which he converted into handsome livery stables (his present premises). In 1878 Mr. Dawson disposed of his premises at Boar's Head Inn, as well as his present establishment in Taylor Street, the latter becoming the property of the Bury and Radcliffe Carriage Company, he going into temporary retirement and removing his residence to Blackpool. To be long idle was not in Mr. Dawson's nature and again he started business in Bury, taking stables in Old Springfield, Chesham, Bury. This business he carried on for four years, and in 1885 he bought the business of the Bury and Radcliffe Company, returning to the premises in Taylor Street which he had founded as a place of business. These premises are of large extent and admirably suited for the trade, having buildings of eighty feet long and sixty wide, and of two storeys in height. The stables, coach houses, harness rooms, and provender stores are equipped in first-class style, and the whole establishment is a picture of cleanliness and careful management. The trade of the firm is very extensive, twenty horses being constantly employed, and there being required a rolling stock comprising two hearses, three mourning coaches, four wagonettes, two clarences, two landaus, five broughams, four dog-carts. Mr. Dawson's establishment is capable of executing any contract, no matter of what magnitude. Mr. Dawson is one of those gentlemen who possess the unconscious gift of making themselves agreeable to their fellows, and having a reputation for his upright manly principles he enjoys a high place in the esteem and confidence of his numerous warm supporters, and a large circle of friends outside of business.

William Lord, Lord Street Boiler Works, Bury.—The most extensive boiler works in the town are those of Mr. William Lord, known as the Lord Street Boiler Works, Bury. The works stand on a level and square plot of land of 3,500 yards, and are bounded on three sides by three front streets. The main boiler shop is 170ft. long by 45ft. wide, which is being further augmented by the erection of an additional shop, 120ft. long by 70ft. wide; there is also the riveting shop, which is 50ft. high. The offices are well lighted and commodious; the clerks' and principal offices being on the ground floor and the drawing office on the first floor. The works are replete with the most modern machinery, including two shell-drilling machines, by Booth & Co., Halifax, to drill boiler shells up to 12ft. diameter with rivet-holes $1\frac{1}{2}$in. diameter; two flue-drilling machines, by Seed & Crawshaw; one plate-edge planing machine, by Bentley & Jackson, of Bury; one plate-bending machine, by Richards & Co., to take in plates 7ft. wide; one punching, shearing, and angle-cutting machine, by Cameron, will punch and shear 1in. plates 24in. from edge, and cut angles 6in. by 6in. by 1in.; one flue-flanging machine, by Booth & Co., to flange flues up to 4ft. diameter—this machine will also turn up the edges of the rings after being flanged; one boiler-shell-riveting machine, by Garforth, with 7ft. gap, and weighing over 25 tons; one flue-flange-riveting machine, by Bentley & Jackson—this machine is portable, has a gap of 5ft., is worked by hydraulic, and is used for riveting both flues and shells; and one screwing machine, to screw bolts and boiler stays up to $2\frac{1}{2}$in. diameter. There are, besides the above, the usual complements of small tools usually connected with a well-appointed boiler works. The works are laid out for the manufacturing of high-class boiler work of every description, including Lancashire, Cornish, marine, and vertical. There is also a speciality in spherical revolving boilers for the paper-makers, connected with which Mr. Lord brought out a valuable patent in 1883. The patent consists of a peculiar-formed manhole frame, which is made of wrought-steel, and forged from the solid plate without welding. This improvement has been the means of bringing scores of orders for the boilers into the hands of the patentee, who keeps a regular staff of hands on this job alone, and boilers are constantly being forwarded to all parts of the United Kingdom, the United States, the Continent, and India. Mr. Lord is a practical man, and can himself do a day's work at any branch of the trade. He served his apprenticeship, and began learning the trade by first heating rivets. He passed all the different stages from a rivet-lad to an angle-iron smith, and has since then had a lot of experience in different ways at home and abroad, as a sea-going engineer in the service of the Australian Steam Navigation Co., as a boiler inspector in the service of the Manchester Steam Users' Association, and also as a boiler works manager for a well-known firm. Mr. Lord has been granted an engineer's certificate by the Board of Trade for foreign service.

F. G. Wilson, Cabinetmaker, &c., 12, Union Street, Bury.—This business was founded in 1854 by the father of the present owner and taken over by the latter in 1878. Mr. Wilson has developed a very extensive trade in several important departments that are more or less connected with cabinetmaking and upholstery, and his name is very widely known not only in the immediate locality but also generally in all parts of the surrounding district. The premises include a spacious double-fronted shop that has a commanding position and makes a first-class display of the various goods incidental to the firm's trade, presenting a very superior and attractive appearance. There is a large supply of household furniture, bedsteads, and bedding of the most superior quality, &c., all manufactured on the premises. The commodious workshop is equipped with all the requisites of the trade and thoroughly adapted to the production of the best class of goods. A very efficient staff is engaged and the work is carried on under the personal supervision of Mr. F. G. Wilson. In addition to the departments indicated above, the proprietor also does a large amount of work in making wire, cane, and Venetian blinds to order. In Agur Street, there is a well-fitted workshop where the French polishing is carried on. The whole of the business is conducted with great energy and ability, and the success achieved is well merited in every respect.

J. W. Watson, Artist and Photographer, The Studio, 2, Garden Street, Bury.—This studio was established in 1873 and is excellently adapted and furnished with all modern appliances for the production of high-class work. The artistic work of painting and finishing in monochrome is executed, and all the productions from this studio are carefully supervised by Mr. Watson, an active member of "The Bury Society of Fine Arts" and an exhibitor at most of their annual exhibitions since the formation of the society in 1876. The artistic work from this studio is well known in the district. Special attention is given to photographing machinery—it cannot be produced in greater perfection than at this studio. The large studio, 33 feet by 15 feet, is very suitable for groups, &c. Mr. Watson has practised as photographer in Bury over twenty years.

Samuel Gregson (Successor to the late S. Preston), Coppersmith, Iron, Zinc and Tin-plate Worker, 30, Rochdale Road, Bury.—This business was established by Mr. S. Preston in Stanley Street in 1848, and on his demise in 1879 he was succeeded by the present proprietor. The premises occupied are three storeys in height with an attractive street frontage. The workshop is commodious and well appointed, with a most efficient working plant, including seven cutting machines and several swizing machines, and a large staff of experienced workmen are regularly employed here in this industry, Mr. Gregson carefully superintending every detail of work. The speciality of this establishment is what is known as a "Lancashire Washer," made on an entirely new principle. The show room contains several of these washers, and a miscellaneous stock of zinc and tin-plate wares, &c., all of which are well worth inspection by shippers and the trade. Another speciality consists in the manufacture of lamps of all descriptions, the hall or reading lamp being a special feature in this branch, the construction of which is so unique and utilitarian as to make it the popular favourite all over Lancashire. In the executive department all kinds of mill work, repairing and otherwise, receive prompt attention by experienced tradesmen. The trade is good all round in the several branches, and of a home and export nature, being well established in both sections of commerce. The proprietor is a practical craftsman, and a gentleman of the highest mercantile integrity and status.

John Slater, Mineral Water Manufacturer, Clay Bank, Bury.—This business was founded upwards of twenty years ago in a district of Bury which was known as Bedlam Green, but the premises were demolished for town improvement purposes, and for the last five years the firm has carried on a flourishing trade in the present premises. These consist of a large brick building of two storeys in height, and measuring sixty feet in length. They are equipped in first class style with all the most approved modern machinery, including Codd's Patent Machines, the condenser generator, filling and washing machines, all by the foremost makers, the whole plant being capable of turning out four hundred dozen bottles of aërated waters every day. This house enjoys a wide reputation for cordials of every description, and their gingerette has won a fame for the firm which extends all over Lancashire. Consequently an extensive trade is done which requires the services of a large staff of hands and several horses and vans. Mr. Slater, who was well known in the trade, and much respected by all who knew him, died several years ago, and the business since his death has been successfully conducted by his widow, a lady who possesses business qualities of a high order, and whose agreeable manner has won for her the esteem of many numerous warm supporters.

Bury Coffee House and Refreshment Company, Limited, 8, Market Street, Bury.—Prominent among the public boons of the town must be enumerated the successful operations as caterers carried on by the Bury Coffee House and Refreshment Company, Limited, whose places of business are at the address referred to and at No. 1, Moorgate, and 21, Rochdale Road, both in Bury, and 12, Crostons Road, Elton. A prosperous business is carried on at all these houses, one of the main reasons undoubtedly being that all the refreshments supplied are always fresh and in all other respects of undoubted quality, combined, of course, with civility on the part of the attendants, and being withal inexpensive. The house opens at five a.m. and closes at ten p.m. every weekday, everything being kept scrupulously clean and in such order as to tempt the greatest epicure to partake of a good meal in the place, much less those whose appetites are sharpened by the natural sauce of hunger. An excellent bill of fare is at all times exhibited, dishes of every possible description being at the disposal of customers, at a cost as small as surprising. All who wish to witness an animated scene should visit these rooms about noon any day in the week when the numerous patrons of the house avail themselves of the opportunity of tasting the excellent dinner placed on the table at fourpence to eightpence a-piece. Ascending to the first floor there are three dining-rooms, one being exclusively set apart for the use of ladies. There are also commodious lavatories, the use of which is entirely free to customers of the establishment. The custom is drawn from all classes of society and very extensive. The general manager is a gentleman of great experience in this line of business, and highly respected by the customers of the restaurants for his careful attention to ensure their comfort on all occasions.

William Kay, Coach Proprietor, Boar's Head Livery Stables, 4, Water Street, Bury.—The history of this concern, although comparatively brief, is one that affords a brilliant example of what may be accomplished by the exercise of energy, ability, and enterprise. The business was founded in a very humble way in 1880 by the present proprietor, who then occupied a yard in the rear of the Church Inn, Elton, and whose stock-in-trade consisted of one horse and two cabs. It was not long before this number was increased, and thence arose a necessity for greater accommodation, wherefore the business was removed in 1881 to Back King Street, Bury. Here it remained until 1883, when Mr. Kay was again compelled to seek more commodious premises, and forthwith transferred his stock to Margaret Street. Finally Mr. Kay removed to the present address in 1886, and here he has acquired a valuable connection and become widely renowned. This rapid improvement reflects great credit upon the energetic proprietor, and as he still conducts his business upon the excellent principles that have conduced so much to his success, the trade is still gradually extending in all directions, and his establishment is one of the best supported in the district. The premises are of considerable extent, and comprise a large yard about 100 feet in length by 50 feet in width, in which may be seen a number of vehicles of all sizes and descriptions, suitable for every class of hire. There is also commodious stabling, lofts, &c., all of which are well arranged, and (what is highly important to the welfare of a business of this description) kept in excellent order, while at the entrance is a well-fitted office. The stock now includes several wagonettes, no less then four broughams, landau, dog-carts, &c., together with three mourning coaches and a hearse. With regard to the latter it may be mentioned that funeral orders are executed at reasonable terms, and with a most commendable regard for the wishes and feelings of the bereaved. Over the yard there is a large workshop in which the proprietor does all necessary repairs, and is thus enabled to keep his vehicles in thorough working order. He has a large number of horses thoroughly up to their work and well kept. A very large trade is done, and the numerous vehicles are in almost daily requisition. Orders are promptly attended, and the business is conducted in a first-class manner that speaks well for the principles of the proprietor.

P. P. Curtis, Letterpress Printer, Bookbinder, &c., "Sun" Printing Works, 5 and 7, Butcher Lane, Bury.—This busines was established in the present premises in the year 1887 by Messrs. P. P. Curtis & Robinson, Mr. Robinson retiring at the commencement of 1889. Mr. P. P. Curtis is now the sole proprietor, and has made his name famous for certain specialities. The "Sun" Printing Works are of large extent, and are equipped in first-class style with all the most approved machines and appliances for executing the most perfect printing work and bookbinding of every description. Besides doing a large trade in general printing and bookbinding, this firm has won a high reputation in the trade for the excellence of its specialties for grocers, tea merchants, drapers, auctioneers, &c., and for the moderate prices charged. Besides having won renown as general printers, this firm is well known as the enterprising publisher and proprietor of the smart little papers now so popular under the titles of *The Household Help and Bury Advertizer*, and *The Household Help and Darwen Advertizer*, which are published monthly and circulated gratuitously. These smart little periodicals, giving humorous sketches, many useful hints for the householder, and serving as a price-list and catalogue of the goods dealt in by the foremost merchants in the localities where they are distributed, are now in great demand by all classes of the people, who feel indebted to Mr. Curtis for this valuable little monthly present. The head of this firm owes his success to his thorough practical knowledge of all the departments of his business, his artistic and literary taste and moderate charges gaining him the respect in which he is held by his numerous warm supporters. Mr. Curtis is also the publisher of the "Reliable" Series of Railway Guides, which are extremely popular in the county.

W. Warhurst & Co., Chemists, 14, Fleet Street, Bury.—At the beginning of this century the late Mr. Thomas Crompton established a chemist's business at 14, Fleet Street, Bury, and after conducting it for many years he retired in order to take possession of the business now established in connection with the *Bury Guardian* and the *Lancashire Echo*. Mr. Crompton was succeeded in the chemist's business by Mr. William Warhurst, who carried on the concern for fifty years, and retired from the business in 1871, being succeeded by his son-in-law, Mr. G. F. Clifton, who still carries on the concern. The premises are well adapted to the requirements of a first-class chemist and druggist trade, and the business done corresponds with the fine appearance of the shop and the ability with which it is conducted. The stock is extensive and valuable, and includes all the drugs and chemicals incidental to this description of business. A special feature is the dispensing of the prescriptions of medical practitioners, which are made up with the greatest care and precision, and medical gentlemen recommend this establishment for the reliability of the purity of the various medicines; at the same time the charges are extremely moderate. The business connections are as valuable as they are long-standing, many of the customers having patronised the establishment for a great number of years. Mr. Clifton takes an active part in the business, and the close attention he has paid to every detail, combined with the accuracy with which all his compounds and prescriptions are prepared, have gained him the favour and the confidence of his large circle of friends.

A. Hindell, Merchant Tailor and Juvenile Outfitter, 27, Rock Street, Bury.—This popular establishment is of comparatively recent origin, having been founded in 1888, and it therefore redounds all the more to the credit of Mr. Hindell that the business has so rapidly developed, and that the firm has become so widely renowned in such a relatively brief period. The premises are well known, and are conspicuous for the elegance of their display, which is of a varied and high-class character, a choice assortment of the most superior goods being arranged and set out with due regard to effect. Mr. Hindell caters to supply the public with all kinds of clothing for gentlemen, youths, and juveniles; and the success that he has achieved in this direction is plainly indicated in the degree of popularity that has been attained. The wonderful point about the system of business adopted is how he manages to supply such superior goods at such remarkably reasonable prices. It is beyond the province of this work to enter into any details of the actual amounts charged in any establishment, and therefore these must be obtained by means of a personal visit to the proprietor, who is undoubtedly in a position to supply the requirements of all sections of the public. Among the most noticeable features of the stock are the various Chesterfield overcoats in Melton, Cheviots, worsteds, &c.; the all-wool milled Melton Chesterfield, the new Inverness ulster, boys' suits and overcoats, black worsted overcoats and suits, and a great variety of similar goods. This establishment also keeps a splendid stock of black worsted suits ready made for mourning orders, or can make to measure on the shortest notice. One of the chief specialities is the suit made to measure in all the newest patterns of all-wool Scotch and Irish tweeds, Cheviots and Venetians, finished in the latest style, and supplied at a price that will bear comparison with any establishment in the United Kingdom. The whole of the business is conducted upon sound commercial principles, and with a spirit of enterprise that has met with its just reward in the large trade that has been developed in all parts of the locality.

E. W. Heywood, Pianoforte and Organ Repository, 12, Haymarket Street, Bury.—This popular house was established by the present proprietor in 1865, and for the past twenty-four years has been carefully conducted. The saloon is handsomely appointed and contains a large and well-selected display of pianos by all the celebrated makers. Those by Collard, Broadwood, Kirkman, Brinsmead, Hopkinson, Justin Browne, &c., are often conspicuous. Mr. Heywood's vast experience enables him to place before the public instruments of the best possible kind in their respective classes. A particularly good selection, however, is found in Estey, Bell, Bridgeport, and other well-known organs, and the trade and connoisseurs will find this line will well repay a visit of inspection. The principal is also the sole agent for the district for Hemingway & Thomas's high-class pianos, which are offered at such quotations as to place the charm of music in every home at a comparatively trifling cost. The highest testimonials can be seen at this house recommendatory of these famous pianos. A large trade is carried on in tuning, in which important branch of musical science satisfaction is guaranteed to all customers entrusting their work to Mr. Heywood, who holds the appointment of tuner to the Athenæum and Co-operative Hall Concerts. Experienced workmen are also at hand to renovate and re-cover old and neglected pianos, which are turned out of hand almost equal to new for all practical purposes. Mr. Heywood also holds the appointment of organist and choirmaster of St. Paul's Church, Bury, and has been engaged for thirty years as a teacher of the organ and pianoforte, in which capacity he is highly respected by the musical *élite* of the town. The *clientèle* is numerous and composed both of the higher class of patrons, and of the very numerous respectable families of artisans with which the town abounds.

A. Horrocks, Ironmonger, 8, Fleet Street, opposite the Parish Church Gate, Bury.—The premises now occupied by Mr. Horrocks were entered upon by that gentleman in 1887, and as he has spared no expense in its fittings they are now among the finest of the kind in this district. The whole establishment is admirably arranged and divided

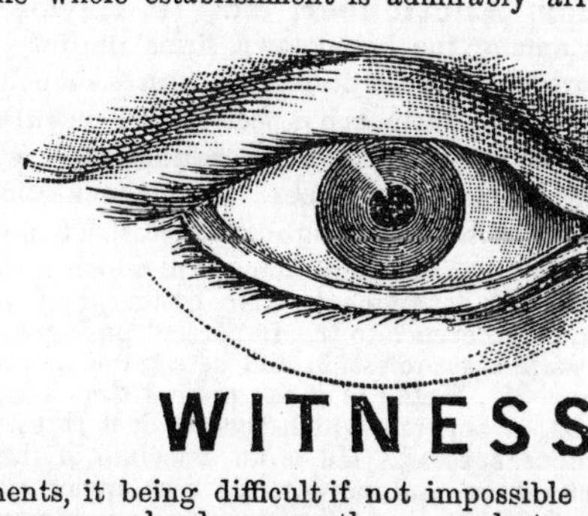

into departments, it being difficult if not impossible to name an article in the ironmongery, hardware, cutlery, or electro-plate trades which could not be had on the premises. A speciality of the house is the "Eye-witness" cutlery. As the trade mark denotes, Mr. Horrock guarantees every piece of the cutlery he sends out. One of the most attractive departments belonging to house furnishing is that connected with fires and fireplaces, where in a most handsomely fitted and arranged room are exhibited marble, granite, enamelled slate, iron and wood, and other mantel-pieces of most artistic designs; kitchen ranges, Abbotsford, Knowsley, Gainsborough, special slow-combustion grates in excellent finish at astonishingly low prices; grates for every room in the cottage or mansion, decorated tiles for hearths, bronze and other chimney ornaments, art lamps, &c. New lavatories with mirrors, baths, hall lamps, chandeliers, gas brackets, splendid variety of gas globes in new tints, and every builder's "requisite." Iron and other bedsteads are also displayed in great variety of sizes and design. There is a valuable stock

of electro-plated goods and a splendid show of useful wedding presents, and fancy articles. An important item which is worthy of special mention is the "Eclipse" draught preventer, a valuable article which will doubtless find its way into many houses. As Mr. Horrocks has a thorough practical knowledge of his business in every detail, and has determined to secure the confidence of every buyer by charging the lowest possible prices, he is rapidly forming an extensive business connection. Mr. Horrocks has a spécialité of his own invention and which he has patented, viz: the "Villa" patent curtain stretcher and one cannot better recommend it than in the words of his circular, "saves its

cost first time of using." Its advantages are that one or more pairs of curtains any size can be stretched and dried quicker than on any other stretcher; the simple arrangement of suspending it to a clothes-line, in or out of doors, makes it most easy and simple to use. It is self-adjusting, and saves the trouble of using the old method of screw pins. It is well finished, and takes up little room when not in use. We can confidently recommend it for home use. Possessing an agreeable courteous manner Mr. Horrocks is much liked in the trade, and his upright principles have gained for him a high place in the esteem and confidence of his numerous warm supporters.

Frederick Gray, Hosier and Outfitter, 17 and 19, Water Street, Bury.—This handsome establishment consists of two large shops, each with three large show windows, the frontage of the whole measuring sixty feet. The shops and showrooms are of handsome proportions, and are fitted up in a very superior style. They are abundantly stocked with every description of hosiery, silk goods, woollens in all forms, and underclothing in all their varieties. The windows are most tastefully dressed; those of No. 19 are chiefly devoted to the display of ladies' apparel and baby linen, and a finer and better assortment of beautiful goods could scarcely be equalled out of London, and not surpassed even there, the quality of every article being of the very best class. No. 17 is more of a gentleman's department, with neckties, collars, shirts, singlets, and pants, and every variety of sundries. The house, however, offers as specialities Dent's gloves, Dent's collars and fronts, the perfect-fitting "Berlin" and "Protector" shirts, and Hygienic underwear for gentlemen, ladies, and children; but in this comprehensive establishment everything is special, and more especially of good quality. Mr. Gray, the proprietor, was for many years connected with one of the best houses in London, and is thoroughly experienced in all the branches of fancy drapery, hosiery, and outfitting. He is well supplemented by a large staff of experienced assistants. This business was established by Mr. Gray so recently as 1885, and he has already made a decided mark in the trade; his uniform courtesy and business tact are aids to him in building up a large and influential concern.

T. Rothwell & Co., Printers and Stationers, &c., Wharfedale Works, Clerke Street, Bury.—This firm was established in 1877, and has obtained an excellent name in the trade and gathered together a thriving and prosperous connection. The premises comprise a large modern brick building, three storeys high, with a frontage of sixty feet, and with all the necessary outbuildings, &c., the whole occupying nearly an acre of ground. The arrangements, internally, are extremely good, and the premises are in every way well fitted for carrying on the whole of the departments of a large and enterprising nineteenth century printing establishment. Every kind of office book, account books, letter books, ledgers, &c., is here manufactured, and the firm has the reputation already of being able to turn out goods in this department equal to anything in the trade. Lithographic work is here also carried on, in all the branches of the art and in the most excellent style. Messrs. Rothwell & Co.'s trade is both of a wholesale and retail character. Every department of the concern is fully employed, and a large number of skilled and experienced hands are engaged upon the finer work of the establishment. The whole of the business is entirely under the management and personal superintendence of Mr. Rothwell, who has had a long and intimate experience in every department of the work, and his work is done with conspicuous ability and business enterprise.

Peter Hardman, English and Foreign Fruiterer, Fish, Game, and Poultry Salesman, 30 and 32, Fleet Street, Bury.—This business, which is the foremost of its kind in Bury, was established at the present addresses in the year 1885, by Mr. Hardman. The premises, which are situated in the oldest block of buildings in Fleet Street, consist of two handsome shops, one being devoted to the sale of fish, game, poultry, ice, &c., and the other, which was formerly used in connection with the public weighing machine, has been most tastefully fitted up as an oyster depôt, with handsome supper-room in the rear furnished with marble tables, and every requisite in first-class style. The trade of the firm is very extensive, and the business connection is of the most

influential order. The fame enjoyed by this firm as the leading game, fish, and oyster house in Bury has been won by Mr. Hardman's long experience in the various departments of the trade, his policy of dealing only in the highest classes of goods and the honourable methods that have always characterised the management of his business. Mr. Hardman is an agreeable, courteous gentleman; and the scrupulous personal care he takes to retain the confidence of his numerous influential supporters, united to his reputed upright principles, have gained for him a high place in their esteem. This establishment is in connection with the Lancashire and Cheshire Telephone Company, and families have thus the facility of direct communication with the house of business. The number is 27.

Samuel Gosling, Tobacco Manufacturer, 8, Union Square, Bury.—This business, although of very recent origin, deserves a prominent place in the mercantile and industrial circles of Bury. Mr. Gosling has been connected with the tobacco-manufacturing trade for some considerable time, and was with the firm of Messrs. F. Smith & Co. about seventeen years. He has lately embarked in business on his own account, and his lengthy experience well fits him to conduct an establishment of this kind. The premises at the above address comprise a building that includes retail shop and factory attached. The former is arranged in excellent order, and is thoroughly adapted to carrying on the trade. Mr. Gosling has the assistance of his own family in this department, they having been brought up to the trade; he is therefore in a position to produce his goods very economically, and supply his customers with a superior quality of tobacco. In addition to the branch of operations connected with the manufacture of tobacco, the proprietor also deals in cigars, of which he has a first-class stock in all the most noted and popular brands. He has endeavoured to adopt a high standard of quality in every department of his trade, and the establishment is daily becoming more popular. Mr. Gosling, having displayed both energy and ability, is well deserving of success.

Mrs. James Hill, Wholesale and Retail Boot and Shoe Manufacturer, 26, Market Street, Bury.—This business was founded by the late Mr. James Hill at premises in Water Street in 1865, and in 1876 the present premises were opened. For some years, too, Mr. Hill carried on a large wholesale boot and shoe manufactory in Stanley Street, where a large number of operatives found constant employment. Since his demise in January of last year, his widow, assisted by her son, has superintended the business. The shop is double fronted, and well appointed, with ladies' fitting room, and a workshop in the rear. All the workmen employed appear to be picked tradesmen, all the work produced being of a high-class quality. The stock held is well selected, extensive, and kept in excellent order for the inspection of patrons. A splendid assortment of ladies', gents', and children's boots and shoes are made in the spacious windows, and their apparent good quality seldom fails to attract the attention of passers by. Reconnoitring the interior an equally good class of goods are to be found in ladies' boots for walking and household wear; while the gents' walking boots for winter use are particularly well worth attention, being made of well-seasoned materials by skilled labour, and offered at quotations that place these first-class goods within the reach of all. Another speciality, too, consists of children's boots and shoes, of which a large variety are always kept on hand. In the measure department, special regard is had to the structure of the foot, whereby an easy and elegant fit is obtained; and all work in this line is hand-stitched, and will bear the strictest scrutiny. Repairs, too, are neatly and promptly executed, the best English tanned leather only being used. The retail business is chiefly of a high-class character, and well established in the town and neighbourhood; and in addition, a widespread wholesale connection is well sustained.

Joseph Mellor, Auctioneer, &c., 10, Haymarket Street, Bury.—Prominent among the best-known firms in Bury is that over which Mr. Mellor presides as sole proprietor with so much ability and well-deserved success. The business has been in existence about seventeen years, having been founded in 1872 by the present owner, who carries on the profession of an auctioneer and valuer. In this connection Mr. Mellor is widely known in all parts of the neighbouring district and has achieved a valuable reputation for the excellent manner in which he has conducted his operations in every department. No better proof of his success could be given than by reference to the important positions he now holds both as connected with his profession and as a valuable member of the general community. Mr. Mellor is at the present time a member of the Bury Town Council, a position which for the last three years he has held with conspicuous success. He is an associate of the Institute of Auctioneers and Surveyors, and has recently been appointed a bailiff by the Court of Record for the issue of distraints under a new act. He is likewise a licensed valuer for transfer, probate, legacy duty, &c., an assessor of fire losses, and an assurance agent, in which he represents several of the most renowned companies. The premises occupied at the above address comprise large and well-fitted offices, where an extensive business is done in every department.

John Nelson, Watchmaker, Jeweller, &c., 2 and 4, Haymarket Street, Bury.—One of the oldest and most popular establishments in the watchmaking trade of south-east Lancashire is that carried on under the title of Mr. John Nelson, which occupies large premises at the above address. The business dates back as far as 1853, when it was founded by the late Mr. John Nelson, to whose energetic ability and excellent management the success that has been achieved may be justly ascribed. Mr. Nelson died in 1876; the business has since been ably conducted by his widow, assisted by her eldest son, Mr. John Nelson, jun. The premises are admirably fitted, all the arrangements being of the best class, and presenting both in their external and internal character a very elegant and attractive appearance. A noticeable feature is the window display, a large stock being exhibited with due regard to effect, and including a great variety of valuable and handsome articles; one of the most conspicuous features is the display of silver services, teapots, cruets, &c., of which there is a very large and varied stock. There is also a valuable assortment of gold and silver watches of the most

superior manufacture, both English and foreign, together with a very fine display of the most artistic productions of the gold and silversmith's art. Gold and gem rings and every description of valuable jewellery is exhibited in great profusion, and the host of fancy articles in this direction renders any attempt at detail quite inpracticable. A large trade is carried on by the firm as watch and clock makers, jewellers, and silversmiths, and in the practical part of the work great attention is devoted to repairs. The house has always been noted for the admirable manner in which the work is completed, and in order to maintain this reputation, Mr. Nelson exercises extreme care in employing only the most skilled and experienced assistants. In the rear of the principal portion of the establishment there is a spacious workshop where an adequate staff is employed under his immediate supervision. The work turned out is of the highest class, thus keeping up the prestige gained by the founder. We may here mention that this firm supplied the mayoral chain to the borough on its incorporation in 1876; it is of a very handsome design and exquisite workmanship, and a fine specimen of the goldsmith's art. Also several gold presentation keys, amongst which may be mentioned the key presented by Mr. Alderman Horridge to H.R.H. Prince Albert Victor on the opening of the recreation ground; also the key presented to Sir Henry James on the opening of the Cobden Club.

Simeon Chatwood, Grocer, &c., 4, Market Street, Edenfield.—This business is undoubtedly the most flourishing and the largest of its class in the whole of the district, and the success that has been achieved is all the more meritorious when it is remembered that, in this part of the kingdom, competition is remarkably keen. Mr. Chatwood carries on a large trade in such a variety of departments that any attempt at graphic description in detail would be impracticable. The numerous branches not only include grocery and general provisions but also boots and shoes, hosiery, Staffordshire ware and a great variety of other goods embracing a very wide scope of operations. The premises occupied are very extensive and are conveniently located in the main thoroughfare of Edenfield. They form a block that has a commanding position at the corner of Gincroft Lane and therefore is one of considerable frontage. The hosiery manufacture is in Gincroft Lane and the goods in this department are far too numerous for detail. The specialities include cardigan jackets, boys' suits, Tam o' Shanter caps, ladies' skirts, children's skirts, children's dresses, under vests, ladies' stockings, gentlemen's stockings, socks and all classes of woolwork. They are machine-made and for both wholesale and retail trade. Mr. Chatwood's motto is that "small profits" will bring "quick returns," and he therefore supplies his numerous customers with the very best quality of goods in every branch of his business at the lowest reasonable price. His system of conducting the business is doing much to secure an even greater connection in the future than he has enjoyed in the past.

T. Ormerod, Wholesale Pork Butcher, 8, Fleet Street, Bury.—One of the most extensive businesses of its kind in the town is that of Mr. T. Ormerod, the founder and sole proprietor, the enterprise having been founded by him in Rock Street in 1868, and was removed to the above address in 1883. The premises occupied is a fine brick structure of three storeys in height, and having a frontage of some thirty feet. The plant attached to the establishment includes all the latest improved machinery for making sauces and other forcemeats, and in addition, a full staff of experienced tradesmen are employed regularly; Mr. Ormerod carefully superintending the general organization of the business. The finest home-cured hams and bacon in Lancashire are cured on these premises, an immense stock being kept on hand to meet the extensive orders received daily. Another great speciality for which the proprietor is noted consists of the manufacture of his famous pork pies, popularly known as the "XL," which are supplied extensively to restaurants and shopkeepers all over the town and far away into the country. Ormerod's genuine pork sausages, too, are quite an institution in Bury, being renowned all over the town for their many excellences—in fact this line constitutes a staple portion of the trade with small pork butchers and others. A very extensive business is also carried on in lard refining, the produce of the house in this line being acknowledged throughout the trade as the best on the market. The trade is wholesale and retail, principally the former, widespread, and particularly well established. The proprietor is a gentleman of great enterprise, and practically acquainted with every branch of the industry his establishment so worthily represents. He has been the recipient of municipal honours, having represented one of the most important wards in the borough on the Town Council until quite recently when he tendered his resignation.

Henry Hargreaves, Ventilating Engineer, Heywood Street Works, Bury.—This business which was established upwards of twenty years since, occupies a large building of two floors. The upper floor consists of Mr. Hargreaves' workshops and office. The leading speciality is the manufacture of a smoke conductor which is an effectual cure for smoky chimneys, and is made upon a greatly improved principle. There is a great demand for Mr. Hargreaves' smoke conductors and this fact alone speaks well for their undoubted efficiency. The proprietor also makes a great number of ventilators adapted to the requirements either of private houses or of business establishments and many of these appliances have been adopted with great success in large buildings both public and private, and notably at the Kendal Public Wash-houses, the Butcher Lane Mills, Bury; the Hope Foundry, the *Bury Guardian* office, and by Bentley & Jackson, engineers, where they have given entire satisfaction. A large amount of work is also done in the manufacture of what is known as the Patent Archimedean Screw Ventilator, and also in many other branches connected with the work in metals. The business is admirably conducted and is one of the foremost in the trade.

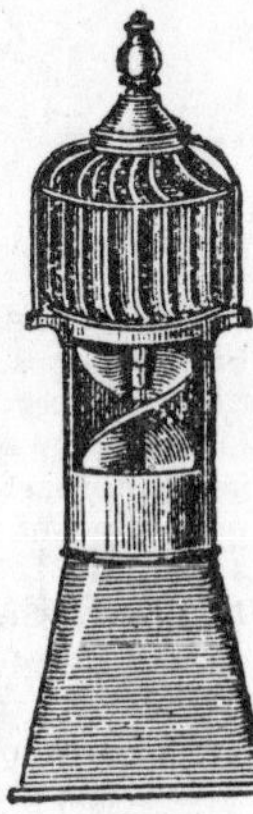

William Walker, Tobacco Manufacturer and Cigar Merchant, 27, Fleet Street, Bury.—This large and influential business was established in 1855 by Mr. Eli Fielding, under whom Mr. Walker was manager up to the year 1857, when he came into possession and added the wholesale department to the then existing retail trade, and subsequently erected the present handsome and commodious building, which has a large and handsome double shop, with exceptionally fine plate-glass frontage; the windows are well and tastefully dressed, and present all the attractive characteristics of a first-class establishment. The upper floor and basement are used for manufacturing purposes, and are replete with all the necessary machinery and appliances for this branch of the trade. In addition to the wholesale and retail trade the firm also sell every description of goods appertaining to a first-class tobacconist, such as meerschaum and briar pipes, cigar tubes, all kinds of fancy articles, pouches, match boxes, and smokers' requisites, all the best-known packet tobaccos, British and foreign cigars of the finest brands, and in splendid condition. The whole of the stock is of first-rate quality and selected with that great care and sound judgment acquired only by long practical experience. A large staff of hands are regularly employed, and the firm are continually covering the whole of the district around Bury. This is the oldest business of its kind in the town and was for many years the only place dealing exclusively in tobaccos and cigars. The business in every department receives the strict personal attention of the proprietor and is conducted throughout with his well-known ability, energy, and enterprise. Mr. Walker, by his well-known integrity, spirited enterprise, and genial courtesy, has secured the confidence and esteem of all classes of his fellow-townsmen.

James Turton, Leather Merchant, "Perseverance" Leather Works, 32 and 34, Stanley Street, Bury, and 17, Church Street, Radcliffe.—The "Perseverance" Works—an honourable and appropriate designation for an establishment with a pushing and industrious gentleman as its directing head—were started by Mr. Charles Turton, Leather Merchant, at 32, Stanley Street, Bury, in 1851. In 1876 he took into partnership his son James, under the style and firm of Charles Turton & Son. In 1885 the senior member of the firm retired, leaving his son sole proprietor. Since the dissolution the business has grown apace, "and finding the original premises too strait," in May, 1888, an adjoining building was added to the original block, giving three spacious fronts, with an entire frontage of thirty-six feet, the basement being divided into two shops. The building is of brick, three storeys in height. There are spacious show-rooms, fitted up with a variety of merchandise suitable for shoe merchants, cloggers, and saddlers. Mr. Turton is a manufacturer of strapping for manufacturing purposes, and keeps a well-

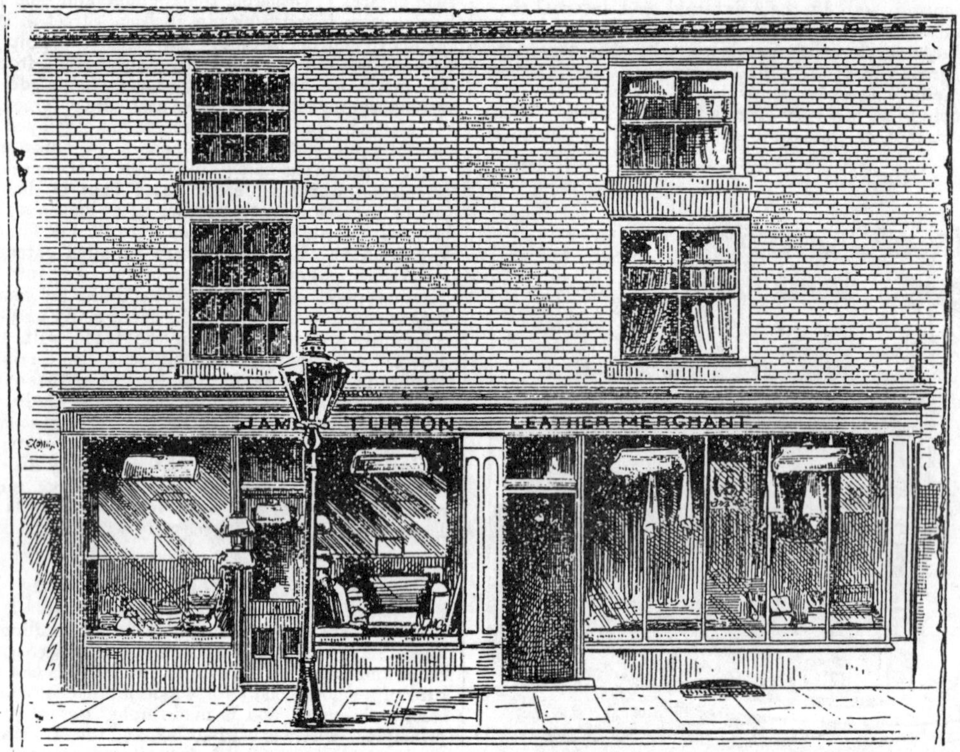

selected stock of strap butts, Welsh roller skins, white, brown, and buffalo laces, oak tanned and green picking bands; also hose piping, india-rubber sheeting, and rings. As a wholesale boot and shoe factor he is in a position for doing a large trade in the district. Mr. Turton keeps abreast with the times, and in addition to the business of leather merchant he has cultivated a business with the youth of the land by supplying them with every requisite for the cricket ground, the football field, and the tennis court. He evidently believes that "all work and no play makes Jack a dull boy." The tourists and travellers bound for distant lands obtain their trunks, portmanteaus, and bags from him, the reason being, no doubt, that his thorough knowledge of leather places him in a position to supply a reliable bag. This has had much to do with his success. Mr. Turton, in January, 1888, opened a branch shop in Radcliffe, where a similar business is carried on. From comparatively small beginnings, we trust the business will still go on increasingly to prosper.

W. & D. Dearden, Tea and Coffee Salesmen, and Family Grocers, Importers of Kiel Butter, 8, Union Street, and 15, Moorgate, Bury.—The important and thoroughly representative business which forms the subject of this sketch is one of the oldest and most noted concerns of its kind in the borough and district of Bury. Its actual foundation must have taken place quite early in the century, for it was a well-established business when it was purchased by the father of the present sole principal upwards of half a century ago. Subsequently the house came into the hands of the late Mr. Joseph Dearden, who carried it on until the year 1882, when he was succeeded by his nephews Messrs. W. and D. Dearden. The present title was then adopted. The present proprietor, Mr. Oswald Dearden, succeeded his brothers, Messrs. W. and D. Dearden, and is now sole principal of the house. He successfully conducts all its affairs under the name and style used by his predecessors, and by his careful administration he fully sustains the reputation of his old and celebrated establishment. For many a year "Dearden's" has been recognised as a grocery institution of high standing and credit by the people of Bury; and residents in this flourishing district have learned to repose every confidence in the house, its goods being always of uniform excellence, while they are in every case sold at the lowest prices consistent with sound quality. In certain lines and departments of their trade Messrs. Dearden hold almost a preeminent position. They are among the largest importers of Kiel butter in the county of Lancashire; indeed, Mr. Joseph Dearden (the late head of the firm) was one of the very first to introduce Kiel butter into this part of England; and the influence of his house has had much to do with the popularising of this excellent product of the Danish dairies. Messrs. Dearden have always been careful to ensure their importations of the commodity in question being of the best quality obtainable, and as a result of this their trade in Kiel butter at the present day is one of very great magnitude. As tea and coffee salesmen this firm have an unsurpassed reputation. They have carefully studied every phase and requirement of this important department, and have achieved unqualified success therein. For many years "Dearden's Teas" have been household words in Bury; and the establishment is especially famous for its unique blend of Indian teas—a production almost unrivalled in the manner in which it brings out the choicest flavours of the finest teas from the gardens of Assam. In all other departments of the grocery trade the name of this house is favourably known. The stocks held are very extensive, and the heavier portion thereof is stored in a commodious warehouse at the rear of the Union Street premises. This warehouse has also a special outfit of machinery for dressing fruit, in which the firm are very large dealers. The chief establishment of the house is admirably situated in Union Street. It is a handsomely appointed and very convenient shop, possessing all the best facilities for the conduct of a large business, and yet in many ways conveying the impression of a sound conservative character, and emphasising the fact that it is the headquarters of one of the oldest trading concerns in Bury. The branch establishment in Moorgate was opened in 1880, and this suburban shop is doing remarkably well. Altogether a better developed or more soundly established business does not exist in Bury. The large trade controlled is entirely retail in character, and partakes of both the "ready-money" and the substantial "family" natures. The connection maintained is a most extensive and valuable one; and, in the hands of Mr. Oswald Dearden, it is safe to say that the reputation of this house and the prosperity it has achieved in a trade career of much more than ordinary length, are sure of all adequate preservation.

PARLIAMENTARY AND MUNICIPAL BOROUGH OF BURY.

Charter Granted September 9th, 1876.

NAMES, DESCRIPTION, AND BOUNDARIES OF THE WARDS,
As defined by the Bury Improvement Act, July 31st, 1885.

CHURCH WARD.

All those parts of the townships of Bury and Elton comprised within the following limits, that is to say, within a line commencing at the centre of Bury Bridge and proceeding in a northerly direction along the centre of the bed of the River Irwell as far as the easterly boundary of the township of Elton, thence in a south-easterly direction along the said township boundary and prolonged in the centre of Paradise-street, thence along the centre of Paradise-street in a south-westerly direction to the centre of Eden-street, thence in a south-easterly direction along the centre of Eden-street, Clough-street, and Rochdale-road as far as the centre of Lord-street, thence along the centre of Lord-street in a southerly direction to the centre of Spring-street, thence in a south-easterly direction along the centre of Spring-street to the centre of Heywood-street, thence in a southerly direction along the centre of Heywood-street to the south side of the Lancashire and Yorkshire Railway, and proceeding along the south side of the Lancashire and Yorkshire Railway in a westerly direction, as far as the centre of Manchester Road, thence in a northerly direction along the centre of Manchester-road and Silver-street to the centre of Bolton-street, thence in a westerly direction along the centre of Bolton-street, and terminating at the centre of Bury Bridge.

REDVALES WARD.

All those parts of the townships of Bury, Elton, Heap, Pilsworth, and Pilkington, included within the Borough and lying south of a line commencing at the centre of Bury Bridge, and passing in an easterly direction along the centre of Bolton-street to Silver-street, thence in a southerly direction along the centre of Silver-street and Manchester-road as far as the south side of the Lancashire and Yorkshire Railway, thence in an easterly direction along the south side of the said Lancashire and Yorkshire Railway to Heywood-street thence northerly along the centre of Heywood-street to Spring Street, thence in a north-westerly direction along the centre of Spring Street to Lord Street, thence in a northerly direction along the centre of Lord Street to Rochdale Road, and thence in an easterly direction passing along the centre of Rochdale Road to the centre of Heap Bridge.

EAST WARD.

All those parts of the townships of Bury, Heap, and Birtle-cum-Bamford included within the following limits, that is to say, within a line commencing at the centre of Heap Bridge and passing in a westerly direction along the centre of Rochdale Road, Clough Street, and Eden Street, to Paradise Street, thence in a north-easterly direction along the centres of Paradise Street, Moorgate, Taylor Street, Kenyon Street, Bridge Street, and High Street, and continuing in a prolongation of the centre line of High Street to the easterly boundary of the Borough, thence along the said easterly boundary to the centre of Heap Bridge.

MOORSIDE WARD.

All those parts of the townships of Bury, Birtle-cum-Bamford, and Walmersley-cum-Shuttleworth, included within the limits of the Borough lying north of Church Ward and East Ward, and east of the centre of the bed of the River Irwell.

ELTON WARD.

All those parts of the Townships of Elton, Tottington-Lower-End, and Walmersley-cum-Shuttleworth, included within the limits of the Borough lying west of the centre of the bed of the River Irwell.

For a description of the limits of the Borough as extended, see the page of Bury Parliamentary Information.

Population in 1881—52,126

NUMBER OF ELECTORS ON BURGESS ROLL.

Moorside Ward	2,476
East "	2,085
Church	1,337
Redvales	1,750
Elton	2,120
Total	9,768
Last year	9,863
Decrease	95

BURY TOWN COUNCIL.

GIVING THE YEAR WHEN EACH MEMBER WILL GO OUT OF OFFICE.

CHARLES BRIERLEY, Esq., MAYOR.

Church Ward.

Aldermen	Robert Peers, 1891, Caleb Amphlett	1894
Councillors	Edward Brierley and Joshua Openshaw	1890
	Ellis Bowker and Kay Kay	1891
	John Parks and Thomas Whittam	1892

Redvales Ward.

Aldermen	Joseph Burrow, 1891, Benjamin Barrett	1894
Councillors	Charles Brierley and James Whitehead	1890
	Jas. K. Butcher and James Maxwell	1891
	Joseph Barrett and William Sykes	1892

East Ward.

Aldermen	Joseph Mellor, 1891. Alexander Robertson	1894
Councillors	John Walker and John Barnes	1890
	Handel Greenhalgh and Roger Peel	1891
	A. F. Bentley and Christopher Talbot	1892

Moorside Ward.

Aldermen	John Ashworth, 1891, John Wardleworth	1894
Councillors	Sam Mosley and Joseph Metcalf	1890
	S. H. Alcock and Peter Smith	1891
	David Eastham and Jesse Meadowcroft	1892

Elton Ward.

Aldermen	George Horridge, 1891, William Smethurst	1894
Councillors	Thomas Hartley and Edmund Whittam	1890
	Christopher Hardman and Thomas Cornall	1891
	James Byrom and Alfred Hopkinson	1892

TOWN CLERK: Mr. John Haslam. ASSISTANT TOWN CLERK: Mr Kay Wild.
BOROUGH TREASURER: Mr. H. Grundy. COLLECTOR: Mr. W. Holt.
SURVEYOR: Mr. J Cartwright, C.E. ASSISTANT SURVEYOR:
MEDICAL OFFICER: H. Ashworth, Esq. SANITARY INSPECTOR—Mr J. Wood
MEAT INSPECTOR—Mr William Heap.
MONTHLY MEETINGS: The First Thursday in each month, at 10 a m.

The members of the Town Council resolve themselves into the following Committees: The Gas Works, the Water Works, the Markets, the Cemetery and Recreation Ground, the Baths and Fire Brigade, the Finance, the Sewering, Paving, and Streets, the Health, the Streets Improvement, the Watch, the School Attendance, the Cattle Plague, Town's Yard, the Parliamentary and General Purposes.

GAS WORKS. Office: Elton. Open from 8 a.m. to 6 p.m. Manager: Mr W. Woodward Collector: Mr. R. Hall

WATERWORKS. Offices: Parsons Lane, Paradise Street, Bury. Open daily from 8 30 to 6. Manager: Mr. Thos. Rigby. Collectors: Messrs. Lancaster & Hutchinson.

BURY MARKET. Opened 24th December, 1839. Inspector: Mr. Walter Hodgson. The Market is open from March 29th to September 29th, both inclusive, every Saturday at 6 a.m., on every other day at 7 a.m.; during the remainder of the year, on every Saturday at 7 a.m., and every other day at 8 a.m. It closes on Mondays and Fridays at 9 p.m., Saturdays at 11 p.m., other evenings at 8 p.m.

BURY CEMETERY. Opened May 21, 1869. REGISTRAR: Mr. H. Pollard. Gardener: Mr. James Wood. The Cemetery is open to the public from 7 o'clock a.m. from May 1st to August 31st; and from 8 a.m. from September 1st to April 30th, to sunset. The Registrar's Office is open daily (except Sundays) from 9 o'clock a.m. to 3 p.m., for the sale of graves, notices of interments, &c. The hours of interment will be, on week days only, from April 1st to October 1st: In the consecrated ground, at 4 p.m.; in unconsecrated, at 3 p.m.; Roman Catholic, 5 p.m. From Oct. 1st to April 1st: In the consecrated ground, at 3 p.m.; in unconsecrated ground, at 2 p.m.; in the Roman Catholic ground, at 4 p.m.

BURY BATHS, ST. MARY'S PLACE. Opened May 2, 1864. Open from April to Nov. from 6 a.m. to 8 p.m.-Sundays from 6 to 8 30. a.m.; from Nov to April, from 8 a.m. to 7 p.m. —Sundays from 7 30 to 9 a.m. Ticket Office closes half an hour earlier. On Thursdays the baths are set apart for females. Superintendent: Mr James Murphy.

BURY FIRE BRIGADE. Superintendent: Mr. E. Geall. Deputy Supt: Stand Pipes, Fire Escapes, and other apparatus are kept at the Gas Works, Elton, and at the Yard in Stanley Street, where the Fire Bell is fixed and Steam Fire Engine kept. Notice may be given at the above-named places, or at the Offices in Bank Street. Stand-pipes are kept at Hampson Mills.

SCHOOL ATTENDANCE OFFICERS: Bury North, Mr T. Rigby; South, Mr A. Bailey.

DISTRICT LOCAL BOARDS.

Members Elected Annually (April), and Serve for Three Years.

RAMSBOTTOM—Chairman : Edward Cunliffe, Esq.

Wards.	Retire in 1890—	Retire in 1891—	Retire in 1892—
Central	H. L. Sladen	Edward Cunliffe	James Pilkington
North	A. Barlow	George Clegg	Robert Holt
East	James Holt	James Duckworth	Thomas Moore
West	J. Pollard	George Whittaker	Sidney Hutchinson

Formed 26th February 1864, Offices: 52 Bolton-street. General Meetings: First Monday in the Month, at 4 p.m. All Committees Meet Thursday before first Monday, at 4 p.m.

The Boundaries of this District were altered by Provisional Order of the Local Government Board dated the 25th May, 1883.

Clerk, W. Wild, Solicitor; Surveyor, Thos. Nuttall, C.E.; Assistant, Jas. Anderton; Medical Officer of Health, Dr. Deans Nuisance Inspector, James Anderton Collectors, Messrs John Hall and Thomas Kay

RAMSBOTTOM BURIAL BOARD—Chairman: Mr H. L. Sladen

Meet every First Tuesday in the Month, at 7-30 p.m. Offices, The Cemetery, Hazlehurst

Retire in 1890—	Retire in 1891—	Retire in 1892—
Rev. W. H. Corbould	Rev. B. G. De Mullewie	R. Mason
J. Strang	Thomas Wrigley	G. J. Cotterill
John Heap	John Booth	H. L Sladen

Registrar—Joseph Lees, The Cemetery.

RADCLIFFE—Chairman : Edward Lowe, Esq.

Retire in 1890—	Retire in 1891—	Retire in 1892—
Edward Lowe	Ellis C. Boardman	John Heap
T. Laurenson	Frederick Scholes	James Ashworth
H. T. Grundy	John Thomas Smith	Richard Walker
S. Walker	William Seed	Joseph Brooks

Formed May, 1866. Offices: Sandiford House. Meetings: First Monday in the Month, at 6 30 p.m. The Members resolve themselves into the following Committees, and meet monthly: Finance, Plans and Buildings, Sanitary, Streets, Lighting, and General Purposes, and School Attendance.

Clerk, James Sharples; Collector, F. Hardman; Engineer and Surveyor, W. F. Pinfold. Medical Officer, Wm. Sellers; Law Clerk, J. P. Monks; Inspector of Nuisances, E. Pearson

WHITEFIELD—Chairman : Joseph Bentley, Esq.

Retire in 1890—	Retire in 1891—	Retire in 1892—
Joseph Bentley	John Slingsby	Mark Hardman
Francis Farrar	James Sellers	F. Wardle
R. Ashworth	Thomas Hardman	J. R. Ragdale
E. Swithensbank	Thomas Mills	George Holland

Formed 1866. Offices: Elms-street. Meetings: First Monday in each Month, at 6 30 p.m.

Law Clerk, Mr J. P. Monks; Clerk and Collector, Wm. Skinner; Engineer, Thos. Thorp; Medical Officer, Dr A. P. Dochard. Nuisance Inspector and Surveyor, J. K. Fletcher

PRESTWICH—Chairman : James Kenyon, Esq.

Retire in 1890—	Retire in 1891—	Retire in 1892—
James Kenyon	John Kelsall	Benjamin Heape
Aaron Bailey	Joseph Barker	James Buckley
Richard Denham Walker	John Cotterill	John W. Thompson
	G. W. R. Wood	W. B. Grindrod

Formed 1867. Offices: Chester Bank. Meetings: Second Wednesday in every Month at 9 o'clock a.m. The Members resolve themselves into the following Committees: Works and Nuisance, and Finance

Clerk, A. W. Grundy, 1, Princess-street, Manchester; Surveyor, Mr Peel; Assistant Surveyor and Inspector, James Mellor, Bury New Road; Medical Officer, Dr Hirst; School Attendance Officer and Collector, Thomas Trickett, Prestwich

1st V. B. LANCASHIRE FUSILIERS.

Head Quarters, Castle Armoury.

Formed 13th, June, 1859; Heywood Corps. July 2nd, 1860—Strength about 800.

Officers of the Battalion—

Hon. Colonel : John Hutchinson, P

Lieut.-Col. T. Pilkington Young, P.S.

Majors: F. E. P. Openshaw & G. E. Wike, P.S

Captain and Hon. Major: H. O. Hutchinson, P

Captains: H. P. Young, P; J. Isherwood, P; John Hall, P; T. Oram, P; F. Watson, J. de R. Openshaw and J. W. Kay

Lieutenants: G. A. Kay, P; W. Oram, E. H. Kay, P; E. H. Milnes

Second Lieutenant; S. Woodcock, Junr

Adjutant: Captain T. Hope Stavert, Leinster Regiment

Quarter-Master: T. Woodcock P.

Surgeon: A. Fletcher, M.D.

Surgeon: G. H. Jameson, M.D.P.

Hon. Chaplain: Rev F. E. Hopwood, M.A

Sergeant Major and Orderly Room Clerk: E. Peregrine, Bury

Quartermaster Sergeant: J. W. Parfitt

Sergeant Instructors: J. Lowe and W. Bibbington

LANCASHIRE FUSILIERS.

BURY REGIMENTAL DEPOT.

20th Regimental District.

Wellington Barracks.

Opened 29th April, 1845.

The Territorial Regiment consists of the 1st, 2nd, (Line) & 3rd (Militia) Lanc. Fusiliers 1st (Bury), 2nd (Rochdale) & 3rd (17th Salford) Volunteer Batts.

Colonel: T. H. Clarkson

Major: R. G. Randall

Captain: C. D. Wallington

Lieutenants: O. C. Wolley-Dod and L. L. R. Samson

Acting Adjutant: Capt. A. Montgomery

Staff-Paymaster: W. Bell (Honorary Major) Army Pay Dept

Quarter Master: E. M. Collins

Surgeon Major, J. Parks, Militia Medical Staff

Chaplain: Rev. R. P. Linfield

Sergeant Major: F. Dunne

Regtl.-Q.-M.-Sergeant: J. W. Young

Quarter-Master Sergt.: A. Smith (Orderly Room Sergeant)

Quarter-Master Sergeant: C. Gollop (Paymaster Sergt.)

3rd Batt. Lancashire Fusiliers (Militia)

Hon. Colonel: J. Ashton

Lieutenant-Colonel: T. Hale

Adjutant: Capt. A. Montgomery (2nd Batt.)

Surgeon-Major: John Parks

Sergeant Major: J. Kingston

Regtl. Quarter Master Sergt: J. Entwistle

Paymaster-Sergt. E. Ash, M.-Sergt.

Sergt. Instructor of Musketry: E. Brazier

Bury Pension District

The Military Pensioners residing in this district are paid quarterly by Post Office Money Orders from the Districts os their late Regiments

Pension Office: Wellington Barracks

Naval Pensioners are paid quarterly in a similar manner but direct from the Admiralty

THE DIOCESE OF MANCHESTER.

In pursuance of an Act of Parliament passed July 23rd, 1847, this Diocese was formed by an Order in Council dated the 10th day of August, 1847.

First Bishop, J. P. Lee, consecrated Jany. 23rd, 1848; died December 24th, 1869; aged 65

Second Bishop, James Fraser, Consecrated March 25th, 1870, died October 22nd, 1885, aged 67

BISHOP AND OFFICERS.

Bishop—Rt. Rev. James Moorhouse, D.D., consecrated May 3rd, 1886

Coadjutor, Rt. Rev. F. A. R. C. Roberts, DD.

Dean—The Very Rev. John Oakley, D.D.

Chancellor of the Diocese—The Worshipful Richard Copley Christie, Esq., M.A. (Oxon), St. James's Square

Archdeacons—Manchester: Ven. G. H. G. Anson, M.A.—Lancaster: Ven. W. Hornby, M.A.—Blackburn: Ven. R. A. Rawstorne

Secretary to the Bishop and Registrar—E. P. Charlewood, Esq., N.P.

Office—51, South King Street, Manchester

SURROGATES.

Bury—Revs. R. Hudson and W. J. Lowenberg

Elton—Rev E. Westerman

Edenfield—Rev. J. P. Yeo

Heywood—Rev A. Redman

Prestwich—Rev. W. T. Jones

Radcliffe—Rev. R. Fletcher

Ramsbottom—Rev. W. H. Corbould

Walmersley—Rev. J. D. Evans

OFFICERS OF THE COUNTY.

High Sheriff: Clement Molyneux Royds, Esq., Greenhill, Rochdale

Lord Lieutenant: The Earl of Sefton, Croxteth, Liverpool

Constable of Lancaster Castle: Lord Winmarleigh

Chancellor of the Duchy: The Right Hon Duke of Rutland, London.

Under Sheriff: Henry L. Wright, Esq., Preston. Acting Under Sheriffs: Messrs. Wilson, Deacon, Wright, & Wilsons, Preston.

Clerk of the Crown: H. Stephens, Esq

Clerk of the Peace: F. C. Hulton, Esq, Preston

County Treasurer: H. Alison, Esq, Preston

Chief Constable: Lt.-Col. Moorsom, Preston

Assistant: Captain Ibbetson, Preston

Superintendent of the County Lunatic Asylum at Prestwich: Henry Rooke Ley, Esq

Superintendent of the County Lunatic Asylum, Lancaster: D. M. Cassidy, Esq.

Keeper of Her Majesty's Castle: Mr W. R. Shenton, Lancaster

Governors of County Prisons: Preston, Mr J. Haverfield; Manchester, Major Preston; Kirkdale, Major Knott

Bridgemaster and Surveyor for the Salford and Leyland Hundreds: Mr W. Radford, Manchester.

Analyst—W. C. Williams, Esq, B.Sc., Dover Street, Liverpool

CORONERS.

Bolton and Bury—S. F. Butcher, Esq., Bury

Blackburn—H. J. Robinson, Esq

Manchester—F. Price, Esq

Rochdale—F. N. Molesworth, Esq

BIRTHS, MARRIAGES, AND DEATHS

SUPERINTENDENT REGISTRAR:
Mr. James Isherwood, solicitor, Union Offices, Parsons Lane

DEPUTY SUPT.: Mr. H. Dickinson

HOLIDAYS.—Christmas Day, Good Friday, Bank Holidays, & Fri. & Sat. in Whit-week

REGISTRARS' HOURS OF ATTENDANCE.

BURY NORTH—Mr. J. Melling, 49, Cateaton-st Daily, 10 to 11 and 2 30 to 4; Mondays 6 to 7; closed on Wed & Sat afternoons

BURY SOUTH—Mr. S. Holt, 6, School Brow Monday and Thursday 10 to 12, 2 to 3, 6 to 7, other days, 10 to 11 only

WALMERSLEY—Mr. J. Nuttall, Shuttleworth, Monday and Thursday, 3 to 7 p.m.; at Baldingstone every alternate Tues., 1 to 2 p.m.

BIRTLE—Mr Geo. Ashworth, Hooley Bridge Tuesdays and Thursdays 5 to 7; Saturdays. 2 to 6 p.m.; last Thursday in the month at the Workhouse, 3 to 4 p.m.

HEYWOOD—Mr. G. Fairbrother, 13, Benfield-terrace, Monday, Wednesday, Thursday, and Friday 12 to 2 and 6 to 8; Saturday, 2 to 7; closed on Tuesdays

PILKINGTON—Mr. J. Lancashire, Overseers' Office, Whitefield, Monday and Thursday, 10 a.m., to 12 noon; Tuesday and Friday 8 30 to 9 30 a.m.; Wednesday 6 to 7 p.m.

RADCLIFFE—Mr. R. Ellerbeck, Sunny Mount Daily, 9 to 10 a.m.; Monday, Wednesday, Thursday, and Friday, 5 to 7 p.m.

ELTON—Mrs. Smethurst, 23, Park View terrace, Ainsworth road, Monday to Friday inclusive, 12 to 1 30 p.m. Saturday 4 to 6 p.m.

HOLCOMBE—Mr. Jas. Spencer, Bolton-street, Ramsbottom, Daily 8 to 10 a.m.

TOTTINGTON LOWER-END } Mr. John Farraday, Tottington Daily, except Tuesday, 9 to 1

HINTS ON REGISTRATION.

BIRTHS—Children must be registered by one of parents within six weeks of birth; after six weeks liable to penalty of 40s. DEATHS must be registered immediately after death, a certificate being obtained from medical attendant. Person registering death to be a near relative, and present at death, or in attendance during last illness of deceased.

When Registrar is required to register birth or death at house of informant a fee of 1s. is payable. Every death must be registered before burial, and a certificate obtained from the Registrar, for neither of which can a charge be made. Section 14 of Friendly Society's Act, 1875, enacts that "No Society shall pay any money on the death of a Member except upon the production of a Certificate of such death under the hand of the Registrar of Deaths.

BIRTHS AND DEATHS, during the Year ended June, 1889.

		Births		Deaths
Bury North District	—	735	—	516
Bury South „	—	569	—	393
Walmersley „	—	159	—	93
Birtle „	—	106	—	242
Heywood „	—	548	—	487
Pilkington „	—	422	—	248
Radcliffe „	—	624	—	355
Elton „	—	420	—	272
Holcombe „	—	296	—	209
Tottington-lower-end	—	191	—	119
Totals		4070		2934
Last year		4303		2835

MARRIAGES			Population
Bury Parish Church	28	—	5443
„ St. John's	40	—	6346
„ St. Paul's	40	—	13225
„ Holy Trinity	30	—	6451
„ St Thomas's	15	—	4468
„ St. Peter's	17	—	3301
„ St Mark's	43	—	—
Elton—All Saints'	52	—	11781
„ St. Stephen's	27	—	—
Tottington—St Anne's	17	—	6773
Holcombe—Emmanuel	23	—	4453
Ramsbottom—St. Paul's	10	—	4286
„ St. Andrew's	...	—	956
Shuttleworth—St John's	10	—	3423
Walmersley—Christ Ch.	12	—	2637
Bircle—St. John's	14	—	2155
Bamford—St Michael	6	—	—
Ashworth—St. James's	3	—	142
Heywood—St. Luke's	20	—	8682
„ St. James's	26	—	7538
Birch—St Mary's	20	—	4439
Unsworth—St. George	2	—	2024
Stand—All Saints'	34	—	5387
Stand Lane—St John's	19	—	4129
Radcliffe—Parish Church	35	—	6178
„ St Thomas's	45	—	6918
„ St Andrew's	18	—	2683
Ringley—St Saviour	6	—	1585
Prestolee—Holy Trinity	7	—	—
Ainsworth—Christ Ch.	7	—	1342
Total,	630		

MEM.—A marriage may be solemnized at any of the above Churches after giving 21 days' notice (providing one of the parties resides in the district of the Church they intend to be married at) at Superintendent Registrar's Office, or by banns as before the passing of the Act.

AT DISSENTERS' CHAPELS AND SUPT. REGISTRAR'S OFFICE.

Mr William Grime, Bury ...	152
Mr. Geo. Fairbrother, Heywood	85
Mr Geo. Ashworth, Birtle ...	23
Mr. J. Spencer, Ramsbottom...	96
Mr J. Lancashire, Pilkington ..	75
	431

MEM.—A marriage may be solemnized at any Chapels licenced for that purpose, after giving 21 clear days' notice at the Superintendent Registrar's Office, on production of certificate. If by licence, one day's notice. The cost of which is £2 14s. 6d. The marriage must take place in the presence of a Registrar of the District or his Deputy

CENSUS—APRIL 4TH, 1881.

POPULATION OF THE DISTRICT, 138,307

		Township
Ainsworth	...	1726
Ashworth	... ...	142
Birtle	... ...	2265
Bury, Males 18482, Females 20803		39285
Cowpe, Newhall hey, Hall Carr		3695
Elton	... ...	11947
Heap	... ...	17733
Hopwood	... ...	4439
Musbury	... ...	1010
Pilkington	... ...	13144
Pilsworth	... ...	785
Radcliffe	... ...	16263
Tottington-lower-end	...	16428
Tottington-higher-end	...	3926
Walmersley-cum-Shuttleworth		5519

BURY PARLIAMENTARY AND MUNICIPAL BOUNDARY,

As Extended by the Bury Improvement Act, 1885, and the Redistribution of Seats Act 1885, Schedule 5.

Starting at the junction of the rivers Irwell and Roach, it runs along the centre of the river Roach, including detached portions of Bury, Pilkington, Pilsworth, Heap, and Birtle to Broad Oak wood, thence along a brook through Smethurst Wood to Rochdale Old Road, and continuing in a line to the centre of the reservoir at Ned Mill, thence in a line by the road to Birtle schools and Mawkin, returning along the boundary of the township of Bury to Holebottom, thence to or near Hercules, Gorsey Brow, Birchen Bower, Bradshaw Hill, and Top o'th' Hill, (including a detached portion at Broadoarr) until the said boundary joins Walmersley, at or near Dark Lane Colliery, thence within the said township, including Longcroft and Mount Pleasant to as far as the junction of the roads at Oldfield, thence along the old road to Bass Lane and following the boundary of the Ramsbottom Local Board district to the point where the same joins the township of Elton, near Chestwheel Bridge, thence within Elton (outside the district of Ramsbottom Local Board) to Daubhole, then between Brandlesome Moss and Woodroad, to and across Brandlesome Road, near Longsight, to the boundary of the proposed Tottington and Elton district, thence along that boundary, via Brandlesome Old Hall (but not including it) and curving by Hopkinsons farm to Kirklees Brook, thence into the township of Tottington at Kirklees Brook wooden bridge, continuing along the footpath on the south-easterly side of Beechwood across the highway on the north-west side of the Lamb Inn to Brickfields (including Bolholt works reservoir), thence in a straight line in a southerly direction to the brook which divides the townships of Tottington and Elton running from Four-lane-ends to Bolholt, thence within Elton along the course of that brook to Four-lane-ends, then to Height Barn, thence by an occupation road to Anthony Fold farm and midway between Bentley Hall and Old Holts farms to the boundary between the townships of Ainsworth and Elton, and following it to the boundary of the Radcliffe Local Board, near Lowercroft reservoir, thence along that boundary, via Moor Nook, Starling, Seddons, and Spring Fold, to Round Oak, then, including a portion of the reservoir, along the embankment and crossing both the canal and river at Hinds Mills into the township of Bury, thence along the left bank of the river Irwell until it meets the river Roach, at the point first described—a detached portion of Radcliffe called "Warthfold," being excepted but including a detached portion of Elton, near Hardys Gate.

BURY ELECTIONS.

1832 December 12 { **First Election for the borough** / **Mr Richard Walker, L, 306** / **„ E. Grundy L, ... 153**

Number of Electors, 539

1835 January 6th { **Mr Walker, L, was returned without opposition.**

1837 July 26th { **Mr Walker, L, ... 251** / **„ James P. Cobbett, L, 96** / **„ Robert Spankie, C, 87**

1841 July 1st { **Mr Walker, L, ... 325** / **„ H. Hardman, C, ... 288**

1847 July 30th { Mr Walker was returned unopposed.

1852 July 11th { **Mr Frederick Peel, L.C., 472** / **Viscount Duncan, L, ... 410**

1857 March 28th { **Mr Robert N. Philips, L, 565** / **„ Peel, L.C. 530**

1859 April 30th { **Right Hon. F. Peel, L.C. 633** / **Mr Thomas Barnes, L, 477**

1865 July 12th { Mr Philips, L, ... 595 / Right Hon. F. Peel, L.C. 572

Number of Electors, 1,313.

1867-8—Number of Electors, 1,455

1868 November 17 { Mr Philips, L, ... 2,830 / Viscount Chelsea, C., 2,264

Number of Electors, 5,583.

1874 February 3rd { Mr Philips, L ... ... 3,016 / Major Walker, C, ... 2,500

Number of Electors, 6,260

1880 March 30th } Mr. Philips was returned unopposed

1885 November 25 } Sir Henry James L ... 3976 / J. Grant Lawson C ... 3787

Number of Electors, 8 214

1886 July 7th. } Sir Henry James was returned unopposed.

Population in 1881—49,746.

Number of Voters on the Register:

1889	Moorside Ward	...	1,842
„	East	...	1,662
„	Church	...	1,122
„	Redvales	...	1,462
„	Elton	...	1,688
	Total	...	7,776
	Last year	...	7,836
	Decrease	...	60

COUNTY MAGISTRATES

HAVING JURISDICTION WITHIN THE DIVISION OF BURY.

	Appointed
R. N. Philips, Esq, D.L.	April 20, 1847
Wm. Fenton, Esq	Feb 28, 1848
Richard Bealey, Esq, Radcliffe	Feb 25, 1856
John Hutchinson, Esq, D.L.	Aug 25, 1858
Jonathan Mellor, Esq, Prestwich	July 4, 1859
O. O. Walker, Esq, D.L.	April 8, 1863
J. J. Mellor, Esq, Stand	April 10, 1867
Edwd. Mucklow, Esq, Woodhill	Oct 18, 1869
Jas. Wrigley, Esq	Oct 18, 1869
E. G. Wrigley, Esq, Broadoaks	Oct 22, 1871
Crompton Hutton Esq., Outwood	April 5, 1875
J. Whitehead, Esq., Elton	April 5, 1875
W. O. Walker, Esq., Bury	April 5, 1875
Saml. Knowles, Esq., Tottington	July 5, 1875
J. S. Walker, Esq., Bury	Jan 10, 1876
Richd. Walker, Esq., Belle Vue	Oct 22, 1877
J. Porritt, Esq, Stubbins	Nov 17, 1877
James Kenyon, Esq, Walshaw	Nov 17, 1877
Richd. Wood, Esq, Heywood	April 8, 1878
Wm. Hartley, Esq., Heywood	Apr. 15, 1878
David Smith, Esq., Heywood	Apr 15, 1878
John Whittaker, Esq., Radcliffe	Nov. 1, 1881
O. O. Wrigley, Esq., Bridge Hall	May 22, 1882
C. Walker, Esq.	May 22, 1882
W. Hartley, Esq., Heywood	May 22, 1882
T. Isherwood, Esq, Heywood	Jan 2, 1884
Adam Crompton Bealey, Esq.	Feb. 21, 1887
Frederick Wrigley, Esq.	...
Henry Whitehead, Esq.	...
John Hamilton Openshaw, Esq.	...
John Brierley, Esq.	...
Thomas Aitken, Esq.	April 11, 1887

CLERK TO THE MAGISTRATES: Mr J. Hall

PETTY SESSIONS held at the Town Hall EVERY DAY, at ten a.m. and for cases within the Borough at one o'clock

THE BOROUGH MAGISTRATES.

Appointment of Borough Bench Dec 1st, 1877

The Mayor: Charles Brierley, Esq.

John O'Neil, Esq, Bury	1877
Thomas Roberts, Esq, Chesham Fields	1877
J. Wardleworth, Esq, Water St	Nov 18, 1884
H. Webb, Esq, Manchester Rd	...
Robert Peers, Esq., Bury	Oct. 20, 1886
Joseph Burrow, Esq, Agincourt	...
Thomas Briggs, Esq. The Wylde	...
Thomas Cornall, Esq, Bury	...
John Halliwell, Esq, Bury	...
Wm. Smethurst, Esq, Elton	...
George Horridge, Esq.	1887
John Barlow, Esq.	August 28, 1888
Adam Fletcher, Esq.	...
Joshua Openshaw, Esq	...
John B. Jackson, Esq.	...

Sessions at Heywood every Wednesday. Clerk, Mr Alfred Wallis

Sessions at Haslingden every alternate Monday. Clerks, Messrs Woodcock.

BURY CONSTABULARY.

Offices, Market Street.

SUPERINTENDENT—Mr John Henderson

Inspectors—W. McQueen & S. Fowler

Sergeants—J. Smith, J. Wood, C. Davidson, D. Ross, J. Lilleywhite, D. Grasswick; Detective-Serg. T. Peebles; Clerk, Sergt. Sinclair

The strength of the force in Bury Division is: 1 Superintendent, 3 Inspectors, 16 Sergeants, 90 Constables; total 110.

INSPECTOR OF WEIGHTS & MEASURES

Mr Superintendent Henderson, who attends on the second and last Tuesday in each month, at 9 a.m., at 3, Thomas Street, Bury, to stamp and adjust weights; at the Police Office Heywood, on the first Wednesday in the months of February, May, August, and November, at 9 a.m.; at the Police Station, Radcliffe, on the third Tuesday in January, April, July, and October, at 9 a.m.; at the Police Station, Ramsbottom, on the third Tuesday in February, May, August, and November, at 9 a.m.; at Tottington on the first Tuesday in January, April, July, and October, at 9 a.m.

QUARTER SESSIONS. 1890.

	Jan	April	June	Oct,
Lancaster...		2	30	13
Preston.....	1	9	July 2	15
Manchester	6	14	7	20
Liverpool	14	22	15	28

The intermediate Sessions are usually held six weeks after the commencement of the regular Quarter Sessions, beginning upon Monday. Annual Session, Preston, 26th June

Adjourned ditto, 11th September

SALFORD HUNDRED COUNTY GAOL AND POLICE COURT.

STRANGEWAYS, MANCHESTER.

Stipendiary Magistrate, J. H. P. Leresche, Esq

Magistrates' Clerk: Fred. Rutter, Esq, Strangeways, Manchester

The Visiting Justices meet at the Prison on the last Friday in each month at 2-30 p.m.

Clerk: Fred. Rutter, Esq

Governor: Major J. W. Preston

Chaplain: Rev J. D. Dreaper

Surgeon: Dr. C H. Braddon

Chief Warder: Silas Denbow

Gate Keeper: Edward Raffell

The daily Court opens at 10-30 a.m

HER MAJESTY'S COURT OF PROBATE.

Registrar: G. Bridgemah Simpson, Esq

Chief Clerk: Mr H. J. Cutter

Second Clerk: Mr R. D. A. Wright

Offices: John Dalton-street, Manchester

Public hours from 10 am to 3 pm; Saturdays 10 am to 1 pm

BURY POOR-LAW UNION.

Population in 1881—129,649

BOARD ROOM—PARSONS LANE.

CLERK—Mr James Isherwood, Union Offices

GUARDIANS.

Meet every alternate Wednesday, at 2 p.m.

Chairman—Daniel Fletcher, Esq

AINSWORTH—J. Greenhalgh, Bull's Head

ASHWORTH—Moses Ashworth, Egerton Arms

BIRTLE-CUM-BAMFORD—J E. Porritt Chasewood.

BURY—Micah Barlow; Joshua Openshaw, Heywood street; J. W. Kenyon, Market-street; Joseph Ashworth, Albion Place; Rev F. E. Hopwood, The Rectory; Roger Peel, Primrose Hill

ELTON—Rev E. Westerman, Elton Vicarage; Christopher Hardman, Crostons' Road

HEAP—Thomas Isherwood, Springfield House, Heywood; John Kershaw, Market Street; Sutcliffe Firth, Hill Street

HOPWOOD—John Tattersall, Holly Bank; J. T. Dawson, Manchester Road

PILKINGTON—John Brierley, Spring Clough; Daniel Fletcher, Back o'th' Moss; Robert Taylor, Moss Lane

PILSWORTH—John R. Ragdale, Whitefield

RADCLIFFE—Thos. Davenport, Black Lane; Wm. Sellers, Clevelands; Joseph Brooks, Bury-street

TOTTINGTON-LOWER-END—Thomas Holt, Walshaw Lane; Rev. J. Shuker, Green Mount; Joseph Strang, Ramsbottom

WALMERSLEY-CUM-SHUTTLEWORTH—Rev. J. D. Evans, The Vicarage; Jas. Holt, Edith Street, Shuttleworth

MEDICAL OFFICERS.

BURY—John Wardleworth, Water Street.

TOTTINGTON, No. 1, T. Mellor, Elton

" No. 2, B. Crawshaw, Ramsbottom

PILKINGTON—K. M. Chisholm

RADCLIFFE AND AINSWORTH—J. G. Saville,

HEAP—Thomas Hunt, Heywood

WORKHOUSE—Thomas Mellor

MEDICAL OFFICER, RURAL SANITARY AUTHORITY—W. H. Barr, Bury L.R.C.P.S.

INSPECTOR OF NUISANCES—Samuel Porritt, Ramsbottom.

RELIEVING OFFICERS.

BURY (NORTH)—John Collins, Canning-street

" (SOUTH)—A. W. Dye, Fishpool

TOTTINGTON—W. Bentley, Elton.

PILKINGTON—W. Hamilton, Whitefield.

HEAP—John Lee, Heywood.

WORKHOUSE—Master, W. H. Bailey

The first Workhouse was hired in 1732.

The old one was built in Redvales in 1775-6.

The present Union Workhouse was opened 21st January, 1857.

From the introduction of Poor Laws to so late as 1822 the poor of the parish of Bury were relieved by the Churchwardens and Overseers. In that year a "Select Vestry" was appointed to assist them, which practice was continued until the introduction of the new Poor Law, Nov. 11th, 1840, after which their duties were gradually transferred to the Guardians.

BURY COUNTY COURT.

Commenced March 25th, 1847. First Court holden April 21st, 1847.

[This Court superseded the Court of Requests, instituted July, 1839.]

Offices, Broad Street; open from 10 to 4, Saturdays 10 to 1

JUDGE—Edwin Jones, Esq.

REGISTRAR & HIGH BAILIFF—Mr Henry Brierley, Bury

DEPUTY REGISTRAR—

SUB-BAILIFFS—Messrs J. Warburton, S Birch, and George Murray

AUCTIONEER AND APPRAISER—Mr James Whitehead

The jurisdiction comprises all the townships, &c., in the Bury Union.

SITTINGS OF THE COURT.

January	13 and	20;	July	21 and	28
February	10	17;	Septembr	15	22
March	10	17;	October	13	20
April	14	21;	Novembr	10	17
May	12	19;	Decembr	8	15
June	9	16;			

Court House, Philips Hall. Hour—9 0 am

COURT FEES.

On entering every case 1s in the pound, and 1s extra in each case where the amount exceeds 40s

Every judgment by consent or by default, one shilling in the pound

For every hearing 2s in the pound

For every summons for commitment, threepence in the pound

Service of ditto, sixpence in each case, if the amount in the original demand does not exceed twenty shillings; one shilling in each case where it exceeds twenty shillings

For every hearing on summons for commitment, sixpence in the pound

For every warrant, one shilling and sixpence in the pound

For every jury, five shillings

The fees on all sums from £20 to £50 calculated as £20; all fractions of a pound charged as an entire pound.

LAND, PROPERTY, AND INCOME TAXES.

DIVISION OF BOLTON—BURY CENTRE.

James Watkins, Clerk to the Commissioners 20, Wood Street, Bolton; Frank Watkins, Assistant Clerk; Surveyor of Taxes for the Parishes of Bury, Tottington-Lower-End, Walmersley and Heap, S. Thorne, Rochdale; and for the Parishes of Radcliffe, Elton, and Tottington-Higher-End, Jno. Walker, Bolton

ASSESSOR AND COLLECTOR—Mr. Franklin Booth, Clough-street.

EXCISE AND INLAND REVENUE OFFICE.—Union Chambers, Union Street, Bury

INCOME TAX—UNITED KINGDOM.

	£	s.	d.
Schedule A.—Land, Tenements, &c.	0	0	6
Schedule B.—Occupiers of Farms, &c	0	0	3
" Scotland and Ireland...	0	0	2¼
Schedule C, D, and E. Income ...	0	0	6

If under £150, exempt; if under £400 £120 allowed.

BANKS IN BURY.

Open from nine o'clock until three, except on Saturdays, when they close at twelve

LANCASHIRE & YORKSHIRE BANK, LIMITED

Established 1872; with which was incorporated March 3rd, 1888,

THE BURY BANKING COMPANY,

Established May 13th, 1836.

HEAD OFFICE—Silver Street.

MANAGER—Mr P. Graham Gow
SUB-MANAGER—Mr T. F. Ridge
LONDON CORRESPONDENTS—Messrs Glyn, Mills, Currie, and Co. and The Alliance Bank Limited.

SUB-BRANCHES:

WHITEFIELD, daily, from 9 30 to 12 30
RADCLIFFE „ 9 30 to 3 0
HEYWOOD „ 10 0 to 3 0
RAMSBOTTOM „ 9 30 to 3 0
On Saturdays from 10 to 12 only
TOTTINGTON—Mondays and Fridays 10 to 1.

MANCHESTER AND LIVERPOOL DISTRICT BANK, LIMITED.

BRANCH—MARKET STREET.

Established 1831.

MANAGER—Mr. John C. Sharp.
ACCOUNTANT—Mr E E Minton
LONDON OFFICE—75, Cornhill

SUB-BRANCHES:

HEYWOOD, daily, from 10 0 to 3 0
Manager—Mr W Barritt
RADCLIFFE, daily, from 10 0 to 3 0
RAMSBOTTOM „ 10 15 to 2 45
On Saturdays from 10 to 12 only

UNION BANK OF MANCHESTER, LIMITED.

CASTLE CHAMBERS, OLD MARKET PLACE.
MANAGER—Mr C B Farr
LONDON BANKERS—Messrs. Glyn, Mills, Currie, and Co.

SUB-BRANCHES:

RADCLIFFE, daily, from 9 30 to 3 0
HEYWOOD „ 9 30 to 3 0
Saturdays 9 30 to 12

MANCHESTER & SALFORD BANK, LIMITED.

Rock Street

MANAGER—Mr James Hyslop
LONDON BANKERS — Messrs. Williams, Deacon, & Co.

BURY BANK FOR SAVINGS,

Silver Street.

Established March 30th, 1822.

ACTUARY—Mr C. M. Merchant.
CASHIER—Mr S. Bailey.

The Bank is open on Mondays, from six to eight; Wednesdays, from two to four; and Saturdays, from two to four and from six to eight Interest allowed, £2 15s. 0d. per cent

BURY DISPENSARY AND HOSPITAL.

Founded March 6, 1829

PATRONS: Right Hon. the Earl of Derby; Edmund Harrison, Esq; R. N. Philips, Esq; O. O. Walker, Esq.
PRESIDENT: Rev F. E. Hopwood, M.A.
VICE-PRESIDENT—Rev D. Walmsley
TREASURER Mr John Hall
SECRETARY: Mr Henry Webb
Res. Medical Officer: I. H. Jones, M.R.C.S., L.R.C.P., Lond.
Assistant: Mr H. C. Sugden, M.R.L.S, L.R.C.P, L.S.A
Honorary Medical Officers: Dr A. Fletcher (Secretary), Dr Barr, Dr Nuttall; Dr Telford Dr Sellers, Dr Lees, Dr Wisken, Dr Crawshaw Hon Dental Surgeon, Dr Wormald

Attendance at the Hospital from 9 to 10 a.m., Dispensary, from 3 to 4 p.m. Sundays, no attendance

BURY LADIES' CHARITY.

PRESIDENT: Mrs. O. O. Walker
SECRETARY: Miss Lomax
TREASURER: Mr Rothwell
SURGEON: Mr Wardleworth
MATRON: Miss Clegg, 13, Hardman-street, Fernhill

General meeting, first Thursday in April.

BURY GRAMMAR SCHOOL.

Originally founded in 1635 by the Rev. Henry de Bury; Re-Founded May 6th, 1726

By the Rev. Roger Kay, then Rector of Fittleton, Prebendary of Salisbury, formerly of Bury. Endowed with two Scholarships, for three years each, at St. John's College, Cambridge, or Brazenose College, Oxford.

Scholarships augmented in 1839 by Dr Wood, Master of St. John's, Cambridge, and Dean of Ely, £500 a former pupil of the school, In 1889 by Miss Openshaw, of Irwell House, £1000, to be called the "John Openshaw Scholarship"

HEAD MASTER—

Rev. W. H. Howlett, M.A., Christ College Cambridge

ASSISTANT MASTERS—

Mr G. Brown, D.Sc., London University
Rev E. Lamburn B.A. London University
Rev G. S. Baker, B.A, London University
Mr R Bulmer, B.A.
Mr E. G. Stubbs, F.R.G.S
Mr A. Nuttall, London University
Mr J C Whitehead, F.C.O,
Mr H. Stott

BURY NATIONAL SCHOOL.

Founded 2nd August, 1748,

By the Hon. and Rev. John Stanley, then Rector of Bury. The early endowment has at various periods been augmented by the Benefactions of the gentry of the town.

The School building in Stanley-street was erected in 1815

Present School, Lower Bank Street, opened Aug. 30th, 1887

MASTER—Mr Thomas Gornall.
MISTRESS—Miss Mills

DISSENTERS' CHAPELS,

DATES OF FORMATION, BUILDINGS, &c., MINISTERS, AND YEAR OF APPOINTMENT.

PRESBYTERIAN.

PRESBYTERIAN (1651) English, at Dundee 1690
Ramsbottom, St. Andrew's, 23 Oct. 1873
W. H. Elliot 17th Dec, 1874
PRESBYTERIAN-UNITARIAN, 1664—1719
Bury, Bank-street, 1837, 22nd Oct. 1852
Douglas Walmsley, B.A, July 23, 1874
„ At Chesham 1882-3,
„ Stand, 1695, R. T. Hereford, Sept, 1885
„ at Ainsworth, 1712-15, enlarged 1773
W. Reynolds, B.A. Sept. 8, 1888
„ at Heywood, 14 Nov., 1860
J. E. Stead, 1886

INDEPENDENT & CONGREGATIONAL.

INDEPENDENT, Walmersley, Park, 1664—22 June, 1798—H. Banks
„ Stand, Pilkington, 1665
A. Anderson, B.A., 16 Feby, 1852
„ Bury, 1790, New-road, April, 1793, 21 Oct 1885
J. M. Simcock, Nov. 10th, 1886
„ Bamford 1800, enlarged 1841
W. McIntosh Arthur, M.A. 1875
„ Bury, Henry-street, 19 Nov. 1807
Chas. Ashford, B.A., Feb. 24, 1876
„ Heywood, 1823, York-st, Apl 1, 1836, June 9, 1869
Silas Rixon 1888
Mission-chapel at Captain Fold, 1872
„ Bury, Shorefields Sept. 1838
Castlecroft, 9 Sept., 1840
H. A. Lawson, M.A., Dec. 22, 1878
„ Radcliffe, 26 January, 1848
H. W. James 1883
„ Tottington, Green Mount, 1866
J. Shuker, 1880
„ Stubbins, 1840, 1867
T. Cain 1865
„ Blackford bridge 1875—Mar. 19, 1889
W. Nicholls

WESLEYAN METHODISTS,

Bury, at Pits-o'th-Moor 1760, in Clerke-st 1785
Union-street, 7th Jany., 1817
Stephen Forrest—George C. Clarke
Mission-chapels at Pits o'th' Moor, 1774—1820—7 Nov. 1853; Birtle. 14 March, 1824; Woolfold, 10 May 1848, Walshaw, 12 July 1843, Elton, April 13, 1882; Russell-st 1884;
Heywood, at Goodshaw-lane, 1792-95
„ Market-st, 29 Dec, 1805—13 June, 1828
12 Aug., 1861
R. Law—R. G Roberts (Castleton)
Castleton 1816—18 April, 1862
Bamford, 1835—28 Jan, 1883; Hopwood 1864
3 Mar, 1872
Tottington, 1823; Summerseat, 23 July, 1847
E. R. Eslick, John Rhodes
Ramsbottom, 1825—22 Oct, 1874—
J. Chapple
Unsworth South, 1808; North, 17 Sept, 1847
Radcliffe Close, 22 Sept, 1839
W. Backhouse, B.A.
Radcliffe bridge, St Paul's
George T. Dixon

METHODIST NEW CONNEXION.

Bury, in Bolton-street, 1813; Heywood-st 12th Feb. 1879
E. Holyoake, 1887
Radcliffe. H. Rowe
Mission Chapel at Ainsworth

METHODIST—PRIMITIVE

Bury 1824, in William-street, 1828-9;
Walmersley-road, 15 Feb, 1866
Wilson Barrett, 1889
Mission-chapels at Summerseat, Elton, and Croft-st
Heywood, 1835, repl. 1872, mission-chapel in Miller-street—J. Prestwich, 1887
Ramsbottom, 1833—1862, mission-chapels at Irwell Vale and Edenfield
Radcliffe, Railway-st 1867—R. Heppenstall

UNITED METHODIST FREE CHURCH

Bury, 1836, North-st, 24 Mar, 1837, 7 Dec, 1864
J. Percival, S. Poad, J. W. Davis, 1888-9
„ Parkhills— 1885;
Mission-chapels at Heap Bridge, ; Limefield, ; Warth, 1870-89; Elton, ; Birtle ; Woodhill, ; Hawkshaw-lane Holcombe Brook
Heywood, 1836, 18 April, 1851—Mission-chapels at Hopwood 1861-2, Bury New Rd. 1871-2 E. Evans, 1889
Ramsbottom, 1836, rebuilt 1874—J. Collinge
IND. METHODIST, Kay St, Bury 1869
FREE GOS. METH, Freetown, Bury

NEW JERUSALEM CHURCH

Heywood, 1828 enlarged 1838
Richard Storry, May, 1861
Pilkington July 28, 1880
P. Ramage, Dec 18, 1887
Ramsbottom 1831, replaced 1876
Bury, Walmersley-rd, 13 Dec, 1860

ROMAN CATHOLICS

Bury, St Marie, 1833 Aug. 10, 1842
M. Byrne, 1880
„ St Joseph's, 1861, Peter-street, 1873
• James Fraser, Nov. 1861
„ Guardian Angels, Elton 1886
B. C. Pozzi 1887
Heywood, 1854, St. Joseph, Oct. 3, 1856
Arthur S. McCann, Oct. 3, 1854
Ramsbottom, 1862, S. Joseph, enlarged 1880
B. G. De Mullewie, Jan. 5, 1869
Radcliffe, St Marie, Hugh Carrol

BAPTISTS

Heywood, Rochdale-road 1834
W. M. Arthur, Jan. 1890
Bury, Providence, Freetown, 8 Oct, 1836
R Moxon, 1880
„ Ebenezer, Knowsley-st, 18 Feb, 1853
B. Bowker, Nov., 1885
„ Chesham, John Harper, 1887
Ramsbottom, 1858, rebuilt 1862
James McCleery, 1889

CHRISTIAN CHU, Rochdale-rd, 13 Sep, 1860
J. G. Brocksbank, Oct. 6, 1888
FREE CH. OF ENG. Tottington, 10 Apl, 1868
F. M. Chetwynd, 1887
WELSH PRESBYTERIAN, Benson-street, 1882
E. Humphreys

BURY AUXILIARY BIBLE SOCIETY.
Instituted 1811.

President: Richard Bealey, Esq., J.P.
Vice-Presidents: Dr A Fletcher, and James Maxwell, Esq
Treasurer: James W. Kay, Esq
Secretary: Rev C. Ashford, B.A.
Depositary: Mr William Wardleworth, 5, Haymarket Street
Meet at the Y.M.C.A. Institute

BURY CHURCH SUNDAY SCHOOL UNION.
Formed April 17th, 1869.

PRESIDENT: The Rev F. E. Hopwood
VICE PRESIDENTS: The Clergy of the Town.
Treasurer and Secretary: F. Calrow, Jun.
The Committee consists of two Teachers from each School in the Union, in addition to the Clergy. General meetings are held monthly, when Model Lessons are given, or papers on Sunday School topics are read.

BURY SUNDAY SCHOOL UNION.
PRESIDENT: Mr. D. Eastham
Vice Presidents: Messrs J. Nuttall & E. Smith
Treasurer: Mr Robert Jackson.
Secretary: Mr Jno. Auty
Meet at the Y.M.C.A. Institute

BURY RAGGED SCHOOL.
Commenced Nov. 21, 1859.
GEORGE ST. SCHOOL opened, March 24, 1870
President: Mr J. Ankers
Committee: Messrs. C. Vickerman, J. Turton, D. Waring, W. Nuttall, J. Rothwell, C. Green and J. Entwistle
Treasurer: Mr. Thomas Pennington.
Sec: Mr T. H. Halsall
Penny Bank Secretary: Mr. T. H. Halsall
Band of Hope Secretary: T. H. Halsall
Day School Mistress: Miss P. Spencer

BRITISH WOMEN'S TEMPERANCE ASSOCIATION.
President—Mrs. Lord
Vice-Presidents—Mrs Harvey and Mrs Davis
Treasurer—Mrs Moorhouse
Secretary—Mrs J. Harvey
Object—To help those who have given way to the vice of intemperance, particularly women, to a better and a purer life.
Meet at the Y.M.C.A Institute

YOUNG MEN'S CHRISTIAN ASSOCIATION, EDEN STREET
Established March 31st, 1875.
Present Institute opened Feb. 26th, 1889
Object: The improvement of the spiritual, mental, social, and physical condition of Young Men.
President: Mr. Samuel Knowles, J.P.
Chairman: Mr James Turton
Treasurer: Mr Charles Green
General Secretary: Mr W. G. Wood
Financial Secretary: Mr Charles Vickerman
Meetings every Saturday & Sunday evenings

BURY ABSTINENCE SOCIETY.
Established 1834.
Temperance Hall opened March 28th, 1874
President: Mr. Adam Ashworth
Treasurer: Mr H. Ashton
Secretary: Mr Albert Sutcliffe
Meet every Thursday evening at 7-30, in the Temperance Hall. Annual Meeting in Dec.

HAPPY HOME WORKING MEN'S TEMPERANCE SOCIETY,
Taylor Street.
Inaugurated March 11th, 1873
Open every evening
Officers change Quarterly

CHURCH OF ENGLAND TEMPERANCE SOCIETY & BAND OF HOPE.
ST. JOHN'S BRANCH, Hornby St. School
President. Rev. R. Hudson. M.A,
Committee. All Teachers who are total abstainers
Chairman: Mr John Parr
Secretary: Mr Jethro Jackson
Meetings about once a month. Annual Festival in October

INDEPENDENT ORDER OF GOOD TEMPLARS.
1077 Happy Home, at New Connexion School, Heywood Street, every Tuesday evening
1133 Hope of Bury, Meet at the same place and day.

BLUE RIBBON TEMPERANCE GOSPEL CLUB.
Union Square, Bury.
Object; To promote and cultivate habits of temperance mingled with strict religious principles
President: Mr. James Nuttall.
Treasurer: Mr T. H. Halsall
Secretaries: Messrs O. Holt & R. Scotson
Open daily. Meetings every Sunday evening at the Institute, Agur-street

INDEPENDENT ORDER OF RECHABITES.
Tents meet every four Weeks.
Tent Daniel, Temperance Hall, Henry-st
Sisters' Hope—Tent No. 1, Limefield
" " 2, Warth Fold
Star of Hope (Juvenile), Temperance Hall

SONS OF TEMPERANCE,
Meet every four weeks.
Happy Home, Happy Home, Fridays.
British Workman, Temperance Hall, Saturdays.

LODGES

IN THE BURY DISTRICT.

District Secretaries are requested to advise the Publishers of any error or change of place, or day of meeting, before 1st of Nov. annually

ANCIENT FREE AND ACCEPTED MASONS.
Meeting Monthly:
Relief (42), Grey Mare Hotel
Prince Edwin (128), Bridge Inn
St. John (191), Knowsley Hotel
Napthali (266), Masonic Rooms, Heywood
Faith (344), Bull's Head Inn, Radcliffe
Merit (934), Derby Hotel, Whitefield
Prince of Wales (1012), Derby Hotel
Egerton (1392), Stanley Arms
Starkie (1634), Railway Hotel, Ramsbottom

CHAPTERS—Meeting Quarterly:
Unanimity (42), Derby Hotel
Prince Edwin (128), Bridge Inn
Beauty (344), Bull's Head, Radcliffe
Naphtali (266), Masonic Rooms, Heywood

KNIGHT TEMPLAR—Meeting three times a year:
Edmund Plantagenet Preceptory, Knowsley Hotel

MARK MASTER LODGES—Meeting Quarterly:
Callender (123), Derby Hotel
Alfred (136), Bridge Inn
Wike (142) Derby Hotel, Whitefield

NATIONAL ORDER OF ODDFELLOWS, BURY DISTRICT.
District Secretary, Mr. Richard Lathwood, 9, Tenters Street, Bolton Street, Bury.
Meeting every four weeks on Saturday:
Loyal R. N. Philips Lodge, Commercial Inn, Spring-street
Loyal Prince Edward, Queen's Arms, Freetown
Loyal Albert the Good, Stanley Arms, Stanley-street
Loyal Earl of Derby, White Lion, Bolton-st
Loyal Trafalgar, Knowsley Hotel
Loyal Love of Freedom, Albion Hotel, Bury
Loyal Rose of Heap, Roach Bank Hotel, Rochdale road
Loyal Spring of Providence; Church Inn, Spring-street
Meeting Fortnightly:
Loyal Sir R. Peel, Royal Hotel, Silver-street

GRAND UNITED ORDER OF ODDFELLOWS,
BURY FIRST DISTRICT.
District Secretary—Mr. Charles Beale, 12, Andrew Street, Bury
Meet every four weeks on Saturdays:
Love of Freedom, Horse and Jockey
Jolly Fullers, Boar's Head, Water Street
Diligent Dyers, Boar's Head, Water-street
Sweet Consolation, Old Blue Bell
Rose of Horncliffe, Royal Oak, Edenfield
Hope of Elton, Dun Horse, Bolton Road
True British Oak, Swan Hotel
*Loyal Princess Alice, Peel Hotel
*Rose of Lancashire, Bridge Inn, Freetown
*Perseverance, Roebuck Inn, Rock Street
* Meet every two weeks
Grand Master's Council, Boar's Head, Water-street
J. Wild, 204, Hornby-st Secretary (Sunday)

BURY SECOND DISTRICT.
District Secretary—Mr. Thompson Horne, 66, Cateaton Street.
Meet every four weeks on Saturdays:
176 St. John's, Hand & Shears, Fleet-st.
640 Rock of Peace, Albion Hotel, Bury
Union Victorious, Black Bull
Radcliffe Pride, Bull's Head, Radcliffe
38 Waterloo, Commercial Inn, Ramsb'tm
180 Good Intent, White Horse, Rawtnstl.
1240 Never Daunted, Hamer's Arms, Summerseat

INDEPENDENT ORDER OF ODDFELLOWS,
BURY DISTRICT.
District Offices—10, Henry Street
Open for business on Wednesday evenings, between 7 30 and 9 o'clock.
District Secretary—Mr Samuel Turner, 14, Cedar-street, Bury.
Lodges Meeting Monthly:
Wilton, Bull's Head, Whitefield
Refuge, Woolpack, Radcliffe
Squire Radcliffe, Bull's Head, Radcliffe
Welcome Stranger, Grant's Arms, Ramsbottom
Virtue, Red Lion, Tottington
Grand Cross, Cricketers' Inn, Limefield
Wellington, District Offices.
Offspring, Church Inn, Spring-street
Improved Philanthropist, District Offices
Prince Albert, Red Lion, Blackford Bridge
Brougham, Swan Inn, Woolfold
Irwell, Boar's Head, Radcliffe
Roach, Boar's Head, Heap Bridge
Henry Ratcliffe of P.G.'s, District Offices
Lodges Meeting Fortnightly:
Bury Improvement, District Offices
Collingwood, Grey Mare Inn, Haymarket-st
Britannia & Shakespeare, District Offices
Lord John Russell, Roebuck Inn, Rock-st
William Fourth, Athenæum

ANCIENT NOBLE

ORDER OF UNITED ODDFELLOWS,

BOLTON UNITY.

District Secretary: Mr John Warburton, 51, Deal-street

Meet alternately, on the second Tuesday in January, April, July, and October, at the following places—

576 Marquis of Lorne, New Inn, Elton

144 Conquering Hero, Black Bull, Stanley-street

Flower of Fishpool, Pack Horse, Fishpool

ORDER OF DRUIDS, No. 1 DISTRICT.

District Secretary—Mr. Geo. Longthorne, 12, Robert Street, Radcliffe.

Meet every four weeks on Saturdays :

Purity, Lord Nelson Inn, Bolton-street
Integrity, New Inn, Crostons, Elton
Antiquity, Dungeon Inn, Tottington
Careful, Half-acre, Prestwich
Industry, Cotton Tree Inn, Moorgate
Royal George, Pack Horse, Edenfield
Industry, Three Arrows, Ainsworth

• Hope, Black Bull, Starling, Elton
• Honour, Cross Inn, Radcliffe

•Are independent of the Order of Druids

ORDER OF DRUIDS, No. 2 DISTRICT.

District Secretary —Mr. Peter Greenhalgh, Church Street, Ainsworth.

Meet every four weeks on Saturdays :

Indicator, Hope and Anchor Inn, Bury
Conquering Hero, Duke Wm., Cockey Moor

THE LOYAL

ORDER OF ANCIENT SHEPHERDS.

District Sec.—Mr. John W. Fielding. 41, Baker street, Elton.

Lodges Meeting every four weeks :

Poor Man's Home, Radcliffe Old Cross
Confidence, Happy Home Rooms, Taylor-st
Welcome Traveller, White Lion Inn
Welcome Gentle Shepherds, Blue Bell Inn
Joyful Shepherds, Turf Tavern, Wash lane
Shepherds Rising the Hill, St. Andrew's School room, Black Lane, Radcliffe.

ANCIENT ORDER OF FORESTERS.

District Secretary: Mr. Edward Ditchfield, 3, Moorside, Walmersley Road, Bury.

Courts Meeting every four weeks :

709 Waterloo Court, Queen's Hotel
3270 Commercial Inn, Spring-street, Bury
3492 Dunn Horse, Bolton Road
5361 Britannia Court, Hand and Shears
Prince Albert, Ashworth Arms, Clough-fold
Mount Nebo, Eagle and Child, Higher Lane, Besses
Welcome Home, Church Inn. Ramsbottom

312 Globe Inn, Woolfold
771 Foresters' Arms, Radcliffe Cross
901 Foresters' Arms, Ramsbottom
1787 Dun Horse, Nuttall-lane, Ramsbottom
2239 Printers' Arms, Tottington
2247 Grant's Arms, Ramsbottom
2422 Victoria, Church Inn, Elton
4769 Grapes Inn, Radcliffe Bridge

JUVENILE FORESTERS' SOCIETY.

Established 1867.

President : Mr. M. Walker

Treasurer : Mr. E. Ditchfield

Secretary : Mr. J. H. Shaw, 5, Garden-st.

Collectors : W. Wilkes, J. Driver and J. Livsey. Number of members about 200. Meet Quarterly

UNITED SONS OF ZEBEDEE,

OR ROYAL ARCH FISHERMEN.

Secretary :
17 Hand and Shears, Fleet-street
19 Grant's Arms, Ramsbottom
23 Horse and Jockey, Edenfield
Meet every four weeks, on Saturdays

LOYAL ORANGE INSTITUTION OF ENGLAND.

BURY DISTRICT.

2 Peel Lodge, Lord Nelson, Bolton St Bury

Secretary, Mr E. Worrall, Denton-street

Treasurer, Mr R. Greenhalgh, Arthur-street, Elton.

HEYWOOD DISTRICT.

13, Sanderson's Heroes, King's Arms

Sanderson's Heroes, Juvenile Lodge, Conservative Club

Meet every four weeks

The District Meetings for 1890, will be held on the Second Saturday in May, and the second Saturday in November,

UNITED ORDER OF CATHOLIC BRETHREN, BLACKBURN UNITY.

Secretary—Mr. Wm. Kenny, 13, Agur St

Meeting every four weeks, on Saturdays, at the Queen's Hotel, Market-street.

B U R Y A T H E N Æ U M

Inaugurated November 23rd, 1853.

PRESIDENT: Mr C. B. Farr
VICE PRESIDENT : Mr S. F. Butcher
TREASURER : Mr C. M. Merchant
SECRETARY : Mr W. W. Crompton
LIBRARIAN : Mr W. Robinson

Subscription, including Telegram Room, 15s ordinary members, 10s ; ladies and minors, 6s

The News and Reading Room is open each day from eight o'clock in the morning until ten in the evening, except on Sundays, when it is closed until half-past twelve. The Library is open every day (except Sunday, Christmas day, and Good Friday) from 3 to 4 30, and from six to nine p.m.

Two Billiard Tables are provided.

Science and Art Classes are held during the Winter Session.

BURY DISTRICT CO-OPERATIVE PROVISION SOCIETY.

Established 1856.

President : Mr E. Sharples
Treasurer : Mr Robert Cronshaw
Secretary : Mr Thomas Boothman
Manager : Mr William Wild
Cashier : Mr E. Lonsdale
Librarian—Mrs Peers

THE LIBRARY contains over 13,000 volumes

NEWS-ROOM open daily from 8 a.m. to 10 p.m. ; Sundays 1 to 8 p.m.

Science and Art Classes are held in Class Rooms during the Winter Session

BURY NATURAL HISTORY SOCIETY.

Established January, 1868, now

LITERARY & SCIENTIFIC SOCIETY.

PRESIDENT—Rev. D. Walmsley, B.A.
VICE-PRESIDENT—Mr Thomas Dearden
TREASURER—Mr Robert Kay
HON. SEC.—Mr Thomas K. Holden.
LIBRARIAN & CURATOR—Mr H. D. Halstead

Began with a roll of 21 members. It now numbers upwards of 40 members. There is a Library in connection with it, containing books relative to the subject of Natural History in all its branches, A Cabinet for objects is added.

Subscription, 4d per month.

Object—The spread of information on the subject of Natural History, Science and Literature

The meetings are held in Girls' High School on the second Tuesday in the mouth, at eight o'clock

BURY MUSICAL SOCIETY.

Established September, 1865.

President : John Barlow, Esq. J.P.
Vice-President : Mr George Openshaw
Treasurer : Mr George Pilkington
Secretary : Mr J. Pollitt, 148, Brook-street
Leader : Mr J. R. Openshaw
Conductor : J C Whitehead, F.C.O.
Rehearsals on Tuesdays at 8 p.m

BURY SOCIETY OF FINE ARTS.

Established 1876.

President : Mr C. C. Grundy, F.L.S., R.S.A., F.C.S.

Vice-President : Mr Croft
Hon. Treasurer : Mr E. E. Minton
Hon Secretary : Mr P. Halliwell

Meetings held in the Society's Room, Victoria Chambers, Rock-street

The Society holds an annual exhibition

BURY PHOTOGRAPHIC AND ARTS CLUB.

Established May, 1881.

President : Mr W. Booth
Vice Presidents : Messrs W. S. Barlow and F. Cooper
Treasurer : Mr J. Newbold, Jun.
Hon. Sec. : Mr F. W. Livsey
Assistant Sec. : Mr Roger Wood, Bolton St.
Council : Messrs. R. Grundy, Junr. C. H. Openshaw, E. W. Mellor and R. Grundy, sen.

Meetings third Wednesday in each month
Annual Meeting on Third Wednesday in October, at 7-30

BURY ANGLING ASSOCIATION.

President—Mr William Nabb

Treasurer and Secretary—Mr Thos Ainsworth

Subscriptions—For the use of two rods, shooting and other privileges, £1 1s.

Season begins April 1st

Object : To preserve fish in the Manchester, Bolton, and Bury Canal Reservoir

BURY CRICKET CLUB.

Established 1845.

President : Richard Walker, Esq.
Treasurer : Mr Herbert Hamer
Hon. Secretary : Mr E. Simpkin
Assistant Secretary : James Wood
Professionals :—G. R. Baker, Lancashire County, A. Smith, and A. Malpass

BURY FOOTBALL CLUB—RUGBY

President : Roger Walker, Esq.
Secretary : Mr. F. Edmondson
Captain : Mr. W. Whittle
Vice Captain : Mr F. Calrow

Ground, Hardmans Bottoms. White and blue Head Quarters : Fernhill Hotel

BURY FOOTBALL CLUB, ASSOCIATION

President : Sir Henry James, M.P.
Treasurer : Mr Harrison
Secretary : Mr J. Melling, 49, Cateaton-st
Captains—J. L. Scowcroft and J. Fitton
Ground, Gigg Lane White and blue
Head Quarters : Coach & Horses, Princes-st

BURY POST OFFICE.—Postmaster, Mr. J. W. Elliott.

Town Deliveries begin at 7 0 and 11 20 a.m., 2 30 and 5 0 p.m. Sundays at 7 0 a.m.

For all Ordinary Business.—Opened to the public at 7 a.m.; closed at 9 p.m. On Sunday it is open only from 7-0 a.m. till 10 a.m.; but the letter-box remains open until 8 p.m.

DEPARTURES TO	Box Closes at
Walmersley, Shuttleworth, Edenfield, Tottington, Heap Bridge, Unsworth, & Birtle	5 45 a m
Manchester, the North, and Ireland...9 15. Oldham ...	10 0 a m
Yorkshire, Midland, Eastern and Southern Counties, London & line of road; Manchester, towns in Lancashire; Liverpool	10 25 a m
Bolton...11 15 Oldham	11 20 a m
Manchester and District, London, South of England, and the Continent ...	12 0 noon
Radcliffe...12 30 p.m. Rochdale	12 45 p m
Bolton, Preston and the North	1 30 p m
Edenfield, Ramsbottom & Bacup...1 45 p.m. Manchester & Surrounding Districts	2 0 p m
Burnley...2 20 p.m. Oldham...2 30 p.m. Liverpool	2 45 p m
Rawtenstall...3 15 p.m Rochdale, Haslingden and Blackburn	3 40 p m
Bolton...4 30 p.m Woolfold and Tottington, Unsworth, Heap Bridge, Walmersley	4 20 p m
Edenfield and Shuttleworth ..4 40 p.m Manchester...4-50 p.m. Wigan ...	5 0 p m
London (night mail) and general despatch ... ... With extra Halfpenny Stamp up to 9 0 p.m.	8 40 p m
ON SUNDAYS—London (night mail), and general despatch ... ... With extra Halfpenny Stamp up to 8 10 p.m.	8 0 p m

COLLECTIONS FROM	ON WEEK DAYS								SUNDAYS	
	am	am	am	am	pm	pm	pm	pm	am	pm
Bass Lane ...	...	...	9 15	...	...	...	...	6 15	...	...
Blackford Bridge SO	...	...	9 40	...	...	...	...	6 45	...	...
Bolton Street ...	5 30	8 30	9 45	11 0	1 0	3 45	6 0	8 [illegible]	5 30	6 0
Bolton Road ...	...	8 15	...	10 30	...	3 0	6 0	7 30	...	...
Bury Bridge RO	...	8 15	9 30	10 45	1 0	3 30	6 0	7 45	...	...
Birtle	...	...	9 30	...	...	...	...	5 30	...	...
Carrfield	...	...	9 45	...	...	3 15	...	7 0	...	6 0
Chesham ... RO	...	8 15	...	10 30	1 0	3 30	6 0	7 45	...	...
Crostons Road ...	...	8 0	...	10 45	12 30	3 0	...	7 30	...	...
East Lanc. Station .	5 30	8 30	9 45	11 0	1 0	4 0	6 0	8 0	5 30	6 0
Edenfield ... SO	...	...	9 45	...	...	...	...	7 45	...	...
,, Market Plce	...	8 15	...	...	...	...	...	7 0	...	...
Ewood Bridge ...	...	7 0	...	...	...	2 30	...	5 15	...	...
Fern Grove ...	...	...	9 45	...	...	...	...	7 15	...	...
Fishpool ... RO	...	8 15	10 0	11 0	12 45	3 15	...	7 30	...	...
Freetown	...	8 15	...	10 45	1 15	3 30	...	7 30	...	...
Greenmount ...	...	...	9 0	...	...	...	...	6 30	...	...
Hawkshaw Lane SO	...	...	8 0	...	..	...	...	6 15	...	...
Heap Bridge SO	...	...	9 45	...	...	...	...	7 0	...	...
Hollins ... SO	...	...	9 30	...	...	...	...	6 30	...	...
Hornby Street ...	...	8 15	...	10 30	1 0	3 15	...	7 45	...	6 0
Knowsley St Station	4 30	8 30	9 45	11 0	1 15	4 15	6 0	8 0	...	...
Leeman's Hill ...	...	...	...	10 15	...	...	...	7 15	9 45	...
Littlewood Cross ...	...	...	10 0	...	...	...	...	7 0	...	...
Market Place ...	5 30	8 30	10 0	11 15	1 30	4 0	6 0	8 0	5 30	6 0
Moorgate ... RO	...	8 15	9 45	11 0	1 15	3 45	6 0	7 45	...	...
Pits o'th' Moor ...	...	8 15	...	11 0	1 0	3 30	...	7 15	...	...
Pimhole Lane ...	5 30	8 15	...	10 45	1 0	3 30	...	7 15	5 30	...
Redvales	5 30	8 30	...	11 0	1 0	3 45	...	7 30	5 30	6 0
Rock Street RO	5 30	8 15	10 0	11 0	1 30	3 45	6 0	8 0	5 30	6 0
Rochdale Road ..RO	...	8 15	9 45	10 45	1 0	3 30	6 0	7 45	...	...
,, ,, Pillar	5 30	8 30	9 45	10 45	1 0	3 30	6 0	7 45	5 30	...
Shuttleworth SO	...	...	10 0	...	...	...	...	7 30	...	5 0
Spring Street RO	...	8 15	9 30	10 30	1 10	3 30	6 0	7 45	...	...
Stanley Street ...	5 30	8 30	10 0	11 0	1 30	3 45	6 0	8 0	5 30	6 0
Tenterden Street ...	5 30	8 30	10 0	11 15	1 15	3 45	6 0	8 0	5 30	6 0
Tottington SO	...	...	9 55	10 15	...	...	...	6 50	9 25	...
Tottington Road ...	...	8 15	...	10 45	12 45	3 15	6 0	7 30	...	...
Union Square ...	5 30	8 30	10 0	11 0	1 30	3 45	6 0	8 0	5 30	6 0
Walmersley Road ...	5 30	8 15	...	10 45	1 0	3 15	...	7 45	5 30	...
Walmersley SO	...	...	9 40	...	...	...	...	6 45	9 40	...
Walshaw-lane ...	...	8 0	...	...	...	...	...	6 0	...	...
Woolfold ... SO	...	...	10 25	...	...	...	...	7 20	9 55	...

POSTAGES.—Letters:—To all parts of the United Kingdom, and the Channel Islands:—

Under one oz. - - 1d	Under four oz. - - 2d	and so on at the rate of ½d. for every additional 2 ounces.
,, two oz. - - 1½d	,, six oz. - - 2½d	

TELEGRAMS—12 words, 6d.; and one halfpenny for every additional word.

FOR INLAND BOOK POST.—One halfpenny for every 2 oz., or part of that weight:—

Under two oz. - - ½d	Under six oz. - - 1½d	and so on at the rate of ½d. for every additional 2 ounces.
,, four oz. - - 1d	,, eight oz. - - 2d	

NEWSPAPERS, duly Registered, ½d each, irrespective of weight, for inland circulation.

PARCELS POST.—For a parcel not exceeding 1lb. 3d., for every additional lb. 1½d. up to 11lbs.

POST OFFICE ORDERS for sums not exceeding £1, 2d.; £2, 3d.; £4, 4d.; £7, 5d.; ex. £7, 6d

POSTAL ORDERS for 1s. and 1s. 6d.. ½d.; 2s. to 10s. 6d. 1d.; 15s. and 20s. 1½d.

STAMP ACT INFORMATION.

O. C. CROMPTON, Fleet Street,

STAMP DISTRIBUTOR.

Bills of Exchange and Promissory Notes of any kind whatsoever (except a Bank Note), drawn, or expressed to be payable, or actually paid, or endorsed, or in any manner negotiated in the United Kingdom; where the amount or value of the money for which the Bill or Note is drawn or made

	£	£	s.	d.
does not exceed		5	0	0	1
Exceeds £5 and does not exceed	10	0	0	2
,, 10 ,,	25	0	0	3
,, 25 ,,	50	0	0	6
,, 50 ,,	75	0	0	9
,, 75 ,,	100	0	1	0
,, 100 ,,	200	0	2	0

And for every additional £100, or part of £100, of the money thereby made payable, 0 1 0

Foreign Bills—Total Duty same as Inland, and can be represented by adhesive stamps.

Persons negotiating Foreign Bills of Exchange without a stamp, or for neglecting to cancel such stamp, are liable to a penalty.

Agreement or Memorandum, or Evidence of a Contract, under hand only, where the matter thereof shall be of the value of £5 or upwards .. 6d.

Receipts given for, or upon the payment of, money amounting to £2 and upwards ... . 1d.

Bankers' Draft or Order, for payment of any sum of money to bearer, or to order on demand ... ... 1d.

Delivery Order, for any goods, Wares, or Merchandise of the value of 40s. and upwards ... ... 1d.

Letters acknowledging the receipt of cash or bills are subject to the 1d. Stamp Duty.

Penalty for giving a receipt without a stamp, £10 under £100; and £20 above that sum.

Penalty for not effectually cancelling or obliterating adhesive stamps when used, £10.

CONVEYANCES, TRANSFERS, &c.,

where the purchase or consideration money therein or thereupon expressed does not exceed

	£	£	s.	d.
sed does not exceed	5	0	0	6
Exceeds £5 but does not exceed	10	0	1	0
,, 10 ,,	15	0	1	6
,, 15 ,,	20	0	2	0
,, 20 ,,	25	0	2	6
,, 25 ,,	50	0	5	0
,, 50 ,,	75	0	7	6
,, 75 ,,	100	0	10	0
,, 100 ,,	125	0	12	6
,, 125 ,,	150	0	15	0
,, 150 ,,	175	0	17	6
,, 175 ,,	200	1	0	0
,, 200 ,,	225	1	2	6
,, 225 ,,	250	1	5	0
,, 250 ,,	275	1	7	6
,, 275 ,,	300	1	10	0
And then for every additional £50, and also for any fractional part of £50		0	5	0

Of any other kind whatsoever, 10s.

MORTGAGE, BOND, DEBENTURE,

		£	s.	d.
For the payment or repayment of money not exceeding .	£25	0	0	8
Exceeding £25 and not exceeding	50	0	1	3
,, 50 ,,	100	0	2	6
,, 100 ,,	150	0	3	9
,, 150 ,,	200	0	5	0
,, 200 ,,	250	0	6	3
,, 250 ,,	300	0	7	6
For every £100, and also for any fractional part of £100, of such amount		0	2	6

Transfer or Assignment of any—

For every £100, or fractional part thereof 0 0 6

LEASE OR TACK

Of any lands, tenements, &c., at yearly rent not exceeding	FOR A TERM. Not exc'd. 35 yrs. or is indefinite. £	s.	d.	Between 35 and 100 years. £	s.	d.	Exceeding 00 years. £	s.	d
£5 per annum ...	0	0	6	0	3	0	0	6	0
Exceeding £5, but not exceeding £10	0	1	0	0	6	0	0	12	0
Ex. £10 but not ex. 15	0	1	6	0	9	0	0	18	0
,, 15 ,, 20	0	2	0	0	12	0	1	4	0
,, 20 ,, 25	0	2	6	0	15	0	1	10	0
,, 25 ,, 50	0	5	0	1	10	0	3	0	0
,, 50 ,, 75	0	7	6	2	5	0	4	10	0
,, 75 ,, 100	0	10	0	3	0	0	6	0	0
For every sum of £50 and fractional part..	0	5	0	1	10	0	3	0	0

Agreement for a Lease same as actual lease.

ESTABLISHMENT LICENSES.

Carriages.—For every carriage with 4 or more wheels, & fitted to be drawn by 2 or more horses or mules or by mechanical power £2 2s.

With 4 or more wheels, and fitted to be drawn by 1 horse or mule only - £1 1s.

With less than four wheels, and fitted to be drawn by 1 horse or mule only - 15s.

Hackney Carriages - - - 15s

Half these rates only charged on Licenses taken out between 1st October and 31st Dec,

Exemptions.—Waggons or other vehicles used solely for purposes of trade or agriculture

Dogs.—For every dog a license of - 7s 6d

Servants.—For every male servant, of whatever age or in whatever capacity, 15s

Armorial Bearings on Carriage, £2 2s.

Do. otherwise, £1 1s.

[These Licenses should be renewed in Jan. each year]

Game.—License to kill game for the year, to expire July 31st - - - - £3

If taken out 1st Aug. to expire 31st Oct...£2

,, 1st Nov. ,, 31st July £2

Occasional Licenses for 14 days £1.

Gamekeepers £2 for the year: they are also assessed as servants at 15s.

Gun.—Every person who shall use or carry any gun, pistol, or other firearm or air gun, is required to hold a license for that purpose, duty - - - - 10s. a year.

[This does not authorise the holder to kill game].

JAMES CLEARY,

General Wood Turner and Band Sawyer,

52, FREDERICK STREET,
BURY.

WRINGING MACHINE ROLLERS TURNED.

Picking Stick Manufacturer.

STOOLS FOR HOTELS & PUBLIC-HOUSES.

None but the Latest Improved Machinery in use at our works, so that perfect reliance may be placed on excellence of work turned out.

ORDERS PROMPTLY EXECUTED. ESTIMATES FREE.

JOHN WHEILDON,

Furniture and General Broker,

65, KING STREET & FAIR GROUND,
BURY.

PIANOS PACKED AND PIANO CASES FOR HIRE.

PIANO AND FURNITURE REMOVER.

All Removals effected with the utmost care and despatch.

CLIFTON AND KERSLEY COAL CO., LTD.,

COLLIERY PROPRIETORS.

COLLIERIES: Clifton, Kersley, and Newtown, near Manchester.

COAL SIDINGS: Unity Brook, near Dixon Fold Station; Robin Hood, near Clifton Junction.

HIGH-CLASS HOUSE COALS.

FOR PRICES SEE LOCAL PAPERS.

ENGINE COALS,

SPECIAL QUOTATIONS WILL BE MADE.

MILLS, WORKS, and PRIVATE HOUSES supplied direct if desired.

The Public are reminded that if they purchase our Coals, they buy at first cost.

OFFICE—

Stanley Chambers, Silver St., BURY.

DEPOT—BUCKLEY WELLS, BURY.

JAMES SEDDON, Agent.

The handloom weavers' cottages had the loomshops on the top floor. Demolished in 1960, they occupied a site at Huntley Brook on Rochdale Road.

A century or more ago John Wild kept the Fox Inn at 23, Eden Street, conveniently sited next door to Robert Chadwick's Walmersley Brewery.

OLD FLEET STREET, BURY.

"The Rock" was the new name given in 1935 to the thoroughfare which previously comprised Fleet Street, Rock Street, Stanley Street, and Water Street.

An early picture of a steam tram by Bury Parish Church, with workmen taking a break from track-laying in the foreground.

BURY AND RADCLIFFE DIRECTORY.

BURY AND RADCLIFFE DIRECTORY.

BURY AND RADCLIFFE DIRECTORY.

J. K. & R. LORD

(Successors to J. & J. LORD, Established 1843),

Barn Brook Boiler Works,

BURY,

Near Manchester.

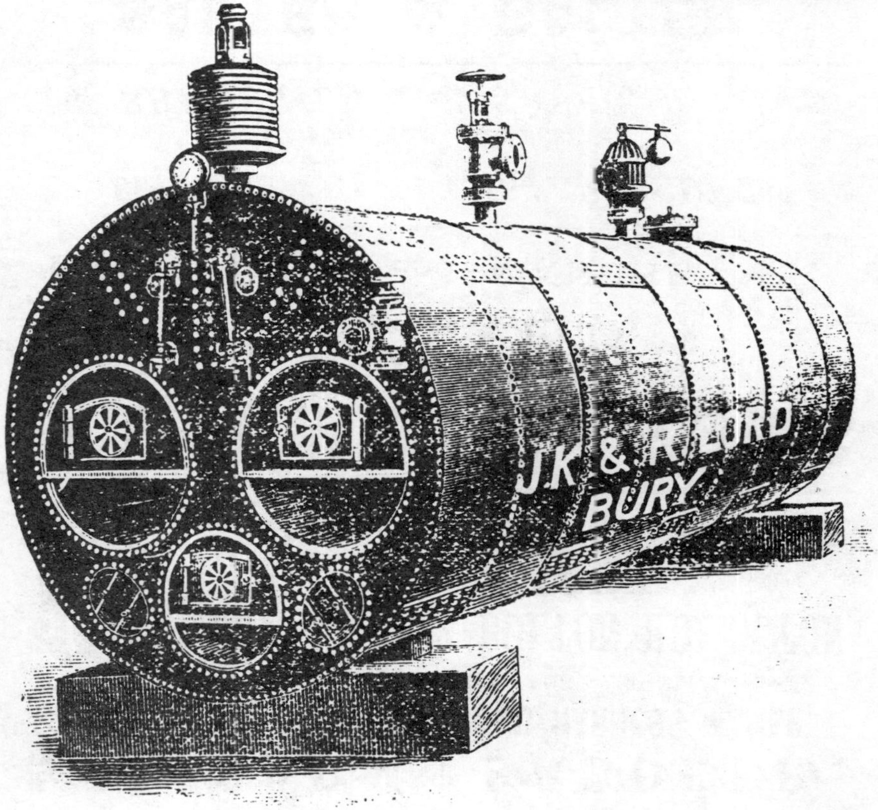

IMPROVED THREE-FLUED BOILER.

Also Makers of High Pressure Lancashire, Cornish, Vertical, and Marine Boilers, from Steel or Iron, with Drilled or Punched Revit Holes, and made with latest improved machinery. Cylindrical and Spherical Revolving Boilers; Kiers; Cased Pans; Tanks for Bleaching Calico, Waste, Rags, Straw and Esparto, Dyeing, Brewing, &c. Wrought Iron or Steel Bridges, Girders, and Beams. Conical and Parallel Tubes for Boilers. Wrought Iron or Steel Tubes and Water Pipes and Columns. All kinds of Boilers Repaired and Re-tubed, and Plate work. All kinds of Boiler Fittings kept in stock.

BURY AND RADCLIFFE DIRECTORY.

BURY BREWERY CO.,

LIMITED,

GEORGE STREET, BURY,

Invite the attention of the Public to their superior

MILD AND BITTER ALES AND STOUT,

All of which are of the highest purity, and supplied in splendid condition.

FOUR-AND-A-HALF

AND

NINE GALLON CASKS

SPECIALLY PREPARED FOR PRIVATE USE.

☞ *ORDERS WILL RECEIVE PROMPT ATTENTION.*

☞ PRICES ON APPLICATION.

Secretary—WILLIAM MEADOWCROFT.

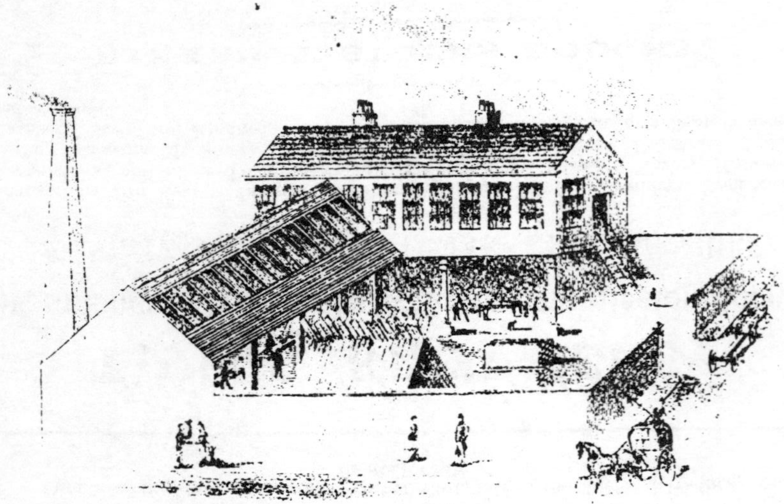

T. ASHWORTH,

JOINER AND BUILDER,

Sydney Street Saw Mills, Bury.

TRAFALGAR HOTEL,

12, MANCHESTER OLD ROAD,

BUCKLEY WELLS, BURY.

Wines, Ales, Stout, & Spirits of the best quality.

CIGARS OF THE FINEST BRAND.

A Comfortable, Convenient, and Well-equipped House.

MRS. MARY HOLT, Proprietress.

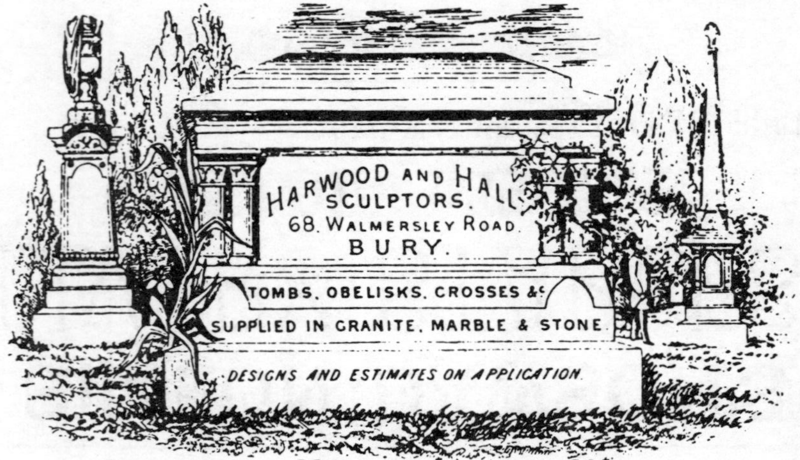

GARFIELD MONUMENTAL WORKS.

Messrs. HARWOOD & HALL,

SCULPTORS,

68, Walmersley Rd., BURY.

IMPERISHABLE INSCRIPTIONS,

Best Material—Good Workmanship Guaranteed.

NOTE:

	£	s.	d.
A Splendid Headstone (with Border-stones), from - - - -	4	10	0
Do. do. in Marble, from - -	6	10	0
Do. do. in Granite, from- -	7	10	0

They are undoubtedly the best to be had at the price, and never fail to give satisfaction.

WE HAVE ALSO A

SPLENDID SELECTION OF TILES

For Hearths, Lobbies, Church-flooring, etc.

BURY AND RADCLIFFE DIRECTORY.

PUBLIC INSTITUTIONS.

BUSINESS.

Banks.

LANCASHIRE AND YORKSHIRE BANK, LIMITED, Bury Branch—Silver street. MANAGER—Mr. P. Graham Gow. LONDON BANKERS—Alliance Bank, Limited. Open daily from 9 until 3, except Saturdays, when the bank closes at 1. SUB-BRANCH at Ramsbottom, open daily from 10-15 until 2-45; Saturdays, 10-15 to 12.

MANCHESTER AND LIVERPOOL DISTRICT BANKING COMPANY, LIMITED—Market street. MANAGER—Mr. John C. Sharp. ACCOUNTANT—Mr. E. E. Minton. LONDON BANKERS—Manchester and Liverpool District Bank, Limited, 75, Cornhill. Open from 9 until 3, except on Saturdays, when the Bank closes at 1. SUB-BRANCH at Heywood—SUB-MANAGER—Mr. W. Barritt—open daily from 10 until 3; Saturdays, 10 to 12. SUB-BRANCH at Radcliffe, open daily from 10 until 3 p.m.; Saturdays, 10 to 12. SUB-BRANCH at Ramsbottom, open daily from 10-15 until 2-45; Saturdays, 10 to 12.

UNION BANK OF MANCHESTER, LIMITED, Bury Branch—Market Place. MANAGER—Mr. C. B. Fair. LONDON BANKERS—Messrs. Glyn, Mills, Currie, and Co. Open daily from 9 until 3, except on Saturdays, when the Bank closes at 1. SUB-BRANCH at Radcliffe open daily from 9-30 to 1-45; Saturdays, 9-30 to 12.

BURY BANK FOR SAVINGS—Silver street. ACTUARY—Mr. C. M. Merchant. CASHIER—Mr. S. Bailey. The bank is open on Mondays from 6 until 8; Wednesdays, from 2 until 4; and Saturdays from 2 until 4, and 6 until 8. Interest allowed—2¾ per cent. per annum.

BANK HOLIDAYS—Good Friday, Easter Monday, Whit Monday, First Monday in August, Christmas Day, and 26th December, if on a Sunday the day following.

Carriers.

BOLTON.—John Ratcliffe, from 121, York street, every day, to Boar's Head.

HEYWOOD AND ROCHDALE.—J. Emmerson, Huntley Brook, Mondays, Wednesdays, and Fridays.

MANCHESTER.—Mark Miles, Castle croft; Manchester Address—46, Shudehill, and 8, Sugar lane; John Leak, Bond street; Nathan Leak, Huntley, daily, to the Hare & Hounds, Shudehill. William Gee, Bolton Road, daily.

RADCLIFFE.—J. C. Ince, from Corn Market Buildings, Haymarket street, on Thursdays.

Post Office.

Broad Street Offices. Joseph W. Elliott, Postmaster—residence: Brierley Street, Fishpool. Open at 7 a.m., and closed at 9 p.m. On Sundays the office is only open from 7-30 to 10 a.m., but letters posted before 8 p.m. will be despatched the same evening. MONEY ORDERS are issued and paid from 9 a.m. until 6 p.m., and on Saturdays from 9 a.m. until 8 p.m. POST OFFICE SAVINGS BANK open at the same hours. TELEGRAPH OFFICE open from 7 a.m. to 9 p.m. daily; Sundays from 8 to 10 a.m. Letters are ready for delivery to private box holders at all hours while the Office is open. POSTAL ORDERS issued from 7 a.m. to 9 p.m., and paid from 9 a.m. to 9 p.m.

Railway Stations.

Lancashire and Yorkshire, Knowsley Street. CHIEF TRAFFIC MANAGER—Wm. Thornley, Esq. SECRETARY—John Harmon Stafford, Esq. PASSENGER SUPERINTENDENT—J. Maddock, Esq., Manchester. CLERK IN CHARGE—Mr. Arrowsmith. STATIONMASTER—Mr. J. Grindrod. GOODS AGENT—Wm. Diggle. East Lancashire, Bolton Street. DISTRICT SUPERINTENDENT—Mr. J. Livesey. CLERK IN CHARGE—Mr. W. H. Hopkinson. STATIONMASTER—Mr. C. Collier.

Revenue.

Government Taxes.

SURVEYOR OF TAXES—Mr. S. Thorn, Baillie Street, Rochdale. ASSESSOR AND COLLECTOR—Mr. Franklin Booth, Clough Street, Bury.

Land, Property, and Income Taxes.

DIVISION OF BOLTON, COUNTY OF LANCASTER, BURY CENTRE.

Mr. James Watkins, Clerk to the Commissioners, 20, Wood Street, Bolton; Mr. Frank Watkins, Assistant Clerk. Surveyor of Taxes for the Parishes of Bury, Tottington-lower-End, Walmersley and Heap, Mr. S. Thorn, Rochdale; and for the Parishes of Radcliffe, Elton, and Tottington-higher-End, Mr. John Walker, Bolton.

CHARITABLE.

Bury Dispensary and Hospital.

PRESIDENT—Rev. E. J. G. Hornby, M.A. TREASURER—Mr. John Hall. SENIOR HOUSE SURGEON—Mr. Isaiah H. Jones. JUNIOR DO.—Mr. L. Hickey. HONORARY MEDICAL OFFICERS—Drs. Fletcher, Telford, Barr, and Nuttall. MATRON (Hospital)—Mrs. Eilbeck. HOUSEKEEPER (Dispensary)—Mrs. Knowles. SECRETARY—Mr. H. Webb. COLLECTOR—Mr. William Clough. The Dispensary is open for the admission of patients every day at 12-30 a.m., except on Sundays. Established March 6th, 1829. The Hospital is open at any hour for the admission of accidental cases. Further information on application to the Secretary.

Bury Friendly Society.

Savings Bank Buildings. PRESIDENT—Rev. E. J. G. Hornby. HON. SECRETARY—Mr. C. M. Merchant. The office is open every Tuesday night from 7 to 8 for the receipt of contributions.

Bury Ragged School.

PRESIDENT—Mr. J. Ankers. TREASURER—Mr. Thomas Pennington. SECRETARY—Mr. T. H. Halsall. SCHOOL MISTRESS—Miss P. Spencer, 38, Audlum Street.

EDUCATIONAL AND RECREATIONAL.

Bury Angling Association.

Fishing Ground: Reservoir off Ainsworth Road, John Scott, keeper. PRESIDENT—Mr. Mark Rigby, Bolton Road. SECRETARY AND TREASURER—Mr. Thomas Ainsworth, Bolton Road.

Bury Athenæum.

PRESIDENT—Mr. C. B. Farr, Belgrave House. VICE-PRESIDENT—Mr. S. F. Butcher, Heywood Street. TREASURER—Mr. C. Merchant, Savings Bank. HON. SEC.—Mr. B. Bolton, Parkfield, Fishpool. ASSISTANT SECRETARY AND LIBRARIAN—Mr. Wilson Robinson, 39, South Garden Street. DIRECTORS—Messrs. B. Bolton, R. B. Hardman, F. Booth, J. Kay, G. Webb, G. Rigby, Wm. Cornall, Rev. W. H. Howlett, M.A.; Rev. J. B. McIsaac, M. A.; W. W. Crompton, Rev. G. W. Löwenberg, M.A.; and J. Veitch. Subscription, with admission to Smoke Room, 15s. per annum; Ordinary Subscription, 10s. per annum; Ladies and Junior Members, 6s. per annum.

Castle Grounds.

Bolton Street. H. Ainsworth, Proprietor.

Bury Cricket Club.

Established 1815. PRESIDENT—Richard Walker, Esq. HON. TREASURER—Mr. P. G. Gow. HON. SECRETARY—Mr. J. Fielden. ASSISTANT SECRETARY AND COLLECTOR—Mr. J. Wood, Cricket Pavilion.

Bury Musical Society.

PRESIDENT—J. Austin Porritt, Esq. VICE-PRESIDENT—Mr. Walter Wild. CONDUCTOR—Mr. J. C. Whitehead, F.C.O. LEADER—Mr. J. R. Openshaw. TREASURER—Mr. J. Pollitt. HON. SEC.—Mr. John Evans, 31, Cateaton Street. LIBRARIAN—Mr. G. B. Crompton.

Opera House and Theatre.

Knowsley Street. Purcell and Revill, Proprietors.

Bury Photographic and Arts Club.

PRESIDENT—Mr. F. Cooper. TREASURER—Mr. R. Grundy, senr. HON. SEC.—Mr. F. W. Livsey, 110, Victoria Terrace, Walmersley Road. Ordinary Monthly Meetings held every 3rd Wednesday in each month. Annual Meeting 3rd Wednesday in October.

Bury Society of Fine Arts.

Established 1876. PRESIDENT—Mr. C. C. Grundy, R.C.A. VICE-PRESIDENT—Mr. Croft. HON. SEC.—Mr. P. T. Halliwell, Stanley Buildings. HON. TREASURER—Mr. E. E. Minton. The Society holds an Annual Exhibition.

MILITARY.

Military Forces in Bury.

Depot, Lancashire Fusiliers, Wellington Barracks.

Colonel—F. L. Edridge, Commanding Regimental District. Major—Randall. Captain Bland. Lieutenants—Goodlake and Read. Acting Adjutant—Captain Montgomery. Paymaster—Major Sutherland. Surgeon-Major—John Parks, M.M.D.

3rd Battalion Lancashire Fusiliers—Wellington Barracks.

Hon.-Colonel—J. Ashton. Lieut.-Colonel—T. Hale, Commanding. Adjutant—Captain Montgomery (Lancashire Fusiliers). Quarter-Master—E. M. Collins. Surgeon-Major John Parks, M.M.D.

1st Volunteer Battalion Lancashire Fusiliers.

Head Quarters and Armoury, Cooper Street, Bolton Street. Strength about 800; six Companies at Bury, and two at Heywood. Hon.-Colonel—John Hutchinson. Lieut.-Colonel Commanding—C. Walker. Majors—F. E. P. Openshaw and T. P. Young. Hon.-Major—H. O. Hutchinson. Captains—G. E. Wike, H. P. Young, J. Isherwood, J. Hall, and T. Oram. Lieutenants—F. Watson, J. de R. Openshaw, R. Nuttall, J. W. Kay, G. A. Kay, W. Oram, and E. H. Kay. Adjutant—Captain C. J. Bloomfield (Lancashire Fusiliers). Quartermaster—T. Woodcock. Surgeon A. Fletcher, M.D. Acting Surgeon—G. H. Jameson, M.D. Hon. Chaplain—Rev. E. J. G. Hornby, M.A. Sergeant-Major—Evan Peregrine. Quartermaster-Sergeant—J. W. H. Parfitt. Sergeant-Instructors—J. Lowe and E. Buffee. Uniform—Scarlet, White Facings.

MUNICIPAL & COUNTY GOVERNMENT.

Bury County Court.

JUDGE—C. Hutton, Esq. REGISTRAR AND HIGH BAILIFF—T. S. Grundy, Esq. SUB-BAILIFFS—Messrs. George Brierley, Samuel Birch, and J. Warburton. (These three persons are appointed as Bailiffs under the Agricultural Holdings Act, 1883.) SWORN APPRAISER, AUCTIONEER, AND BROKER—Mr. J. Whitehead, 4, Agur street. OFFICES—14, Union street, Bury, open from 10 until 4; Saturdays, from 10 till 1. COURT HOUSE—Philips Hall, Bury. HOUR—9-30 a.m.

Municipal Officers.

TOWN CLERK—Mr. Sep. J. Thorp. DEPUTY TOWN CLERK—Mr. Kay Wild. SURVEYOR—Mr. Joshua Cartwright, C.E. SURVEYOR'S ASSISTANT—Mr. J. Cook. BOROUGH ACCOUNTANTS—Messrs. Hamer and Scholes, Fleet street. BOROUGH TREASURER—Mr. H. Grundy. COLLECTOR—Mr. W. Holt. MEDICAL OFFICER—Mr. H. Ashworth. INSPECTOR UNDER CONTAGIOUS DISEASES (ANIMALS) ACT—Mr. Superintendent Henderson. NUISANCE INSPECTOR—Mr. W. Wilkinson, Inspector of Explosives, Petroleum, Canal Boats, and Assistant Inspector under Contagious Diseases (Animals) Act, Canning street. INSPECTOR OF MEAT—Mr. William Heap, Assistant Inspector under Contagious Diseases (Animals) Act. COMMON LODGING HOUSE INSPECTOR—Mr. W. Wilkinson. GAS WORKS MANAGER—Mr. W. Woodward. GAS RENT COLLECTOR—Mr. R. Hall. BATHS SUPERINTENDENT—Mr. James Murphy. CEMETERY REGISTRAR—Mr. Henry Pollard. GARDENER—Mr. James Wood. WATERWORKS MANAGER—Mr. Thomas Rigby. COLLECTORS—Messrs. Lancaster and Hutchinson, Bury; J. Clarke, Rawstenstall. MARKET SUPERINTENDENT—Mr. Walter Hodgson. ASSISTANT—Mr. T. Robinson. SCHOOL ATTENDANCE OFFICERS—Messrs. A. Bailey and T. Rigby.

Bury Constabulary.

Superintendent—Mr. J. Henderson. *Inspectors*—McQueen, 9, Horne street; and Fowler, 12, Bolton road. *Sergeants*—J. Smith, 47, Oxford street; John Lallywhite, 11, Garston street; D. Ross, 58, Frederick street; Donald Grassick, 1, Thomas street; and Jas. Wood, 48, North street; Thos. Stroyan, 22, Lord street. *Detective Sergeant*—Thomas Peebles, 40, Manchester road; *Clerks*—Wm. Sinclair, 17, Dawson street, and D. Keith, Culroes.

Sessions Room, Town Hall—County Petty Sessions held daily at 10 o'clock in the forenoon, and Borough Sessions daily (Monday and Thursday at one o'clock in the afternoon, and other days at 11 a.m.)

Police Constables—Angus W., 45 Wellington-st.; Aspden R., 3 Thomas-st.; Archer W., Town Hall; Boland Thos., Paradise Station; Bowen Chas., 14 Duckworth-st; Bremner Chas., 14 St. Anne's-st.; Brown Alban, 81 Walshaw-rd.; Burns Geo., Gigg; Cornwell Jas., 17 Duckworth-st.; Crompton J., 3 Thomas-st.; Dewer J. P., Victoria Terrace; Dillon John P., 76 Georgiana-st.; Elford J., 49 Taylor-st.; Green P., Little Bridge; Halstead Evan, 51 Hamilton-st.; Hillaway James, 4 Parsonage-st.; Hindle Wm., Manchester-rd.; Hodkinson Robt., Culroes; Holt Chas., Paradise Station; Johnson Jas., 31 Chester-st; Keith David, Culroes; Lewis D., Paradise Station; McQueen M., 9 Latham-st.; McLellan Alexr., 3 Thomas-st.; Marshall J., 119 Brierley-st.; Mathinson D., 80 Walshaw-rd.; Morris Thomas, 18 Duckworth-st.; Morris Wm., Pig's Lee; Murphy Wm., 21 Geoffrey-st.; Nation Hy., 226 Tottington road; Parker Arthur, Paradise Station; Peterson J. W., 9 Church View; Potts Tom, 1 Thomas-st.; Robinson George, 1 Thomas-st.; Smith Silas, Fairfield; Sollitt Hy., 39 Warth fold; Stevens Hy., Coach and Horses; Stobbs Jas., Paradise Station; Swainbank C., Paradise Station; Taylor John, 25 Ingham-st.; Turner Robt., Paradise Station, Wallbank Thos., Limefield, Willcock Thos., 45 Oxford-st.

The Cemetery.

Registrar—Henry Pollard. *Gardener*—James Wood. The Cemetery is open to the public from 7 a.m. to 9 p.m., from May 1st to August 30th; and from 8 a.m. to sunset, from September 1st to April 30th. The Registrar's Office at the Cemetery is open daily (except Sundays) from 9 a.m. to 3 p.m., for the sale of graves, notice of interments, &c.

Fire Brigade.

SUPERINTENDENT—Mr. Edward Geall, Fire Station, Stanley Street. The Steam Fire Engine, Hose Carrier, and Fire Escape are kept at the Fire Station, Stanley Street; Fire Escape and Hose Carrier at the Gas Works, Elton. The Fire Station, Stanley Street, is in communication with the Central Police Station by Telephone, with the Gas Works, and (by Electric Alarm Bells) with the Firemen's houses in Paradise Street, and Elton.

The Markets.

INSPECTOR—Wm. Hodgson. *Assistant*—T. Robinson.

The Public Baths.

St. Mary's Place. MANAGER—James Murphy. Open in the summer season at 6 a.m., and closed at 8 p.m.; winter season open at 8 a.m., and closed 7 p.m. The whole of the baths are set apart for females on Thursday in each week.

Weights and Measures.

INSPECTOR—Mr. John Henderson, Superintendent of Police, who attends on the second and last Tuesday in each month, at 3, Thomas Street, to stamp and adjust weights.

Bury Poor-Law Union

BOARD ROOM—Parson's Lane. Day of Meeting, every alternate Wednesday, at 2 p.m. CLERK—Mr. James Isherwood, Hopwood. OFFICES—Parsons Lane. ASSISTANT OVERSEER—Mr. James Farrar. COLLECTOR—Mr. William Grime.

Medical Officers.

Bury—John Wardleworth, Water Street. *Tottington*—No. 1—Thomas Mellor, Elton. *Tottington*—No. 2—B. Cawshaw, Ramsbottom. *Pilkington*—A. B. Telford. *Radcliffe and Ainsworth*—J. G. Saville. *Heap*—A. Chadwick, Heywood. *Workhouse*—Thomas Mellor. *Rural Sanitary Authority*—W. H. Barr, Bury. *Master of Workhouse*—W. H. Bailey. *School Attendance and Enquiry Officer*—*Tottington District*—Azariah Holding, Holcombe Brook. *Pilkington District*—John Crawshaw, George Street, Whitefield. *Heap District*—Edward Milne, Hind Hill Street, Heywood.

Relieving Officers.

Bury North—John Collins, 59, Canning Street, School Enquiry Officer. *Bury South*—A. W. Dye, Fishpool, School Enquiry Officer. *Tottington*—W. Bentley, Crostons Road, Elton. *Pilkington*—Christopher Wilcock, Whitefield. *Heap*—John Lee, Heywood.

Registrars of Births, Deaths, and Marriages.

Superintendent Registrar—Wm. Harper, Esq., Solicitor, 13, Broad Street, Bury. *Deputy Superintendent*—Mr. H. Dickinson, 13 Broad Street, Bury. *Registrars of Marriages*—Mr. William Grime, 17 Parsons Lane, Bury; Mr. Geo. Ashworth, Hooley Bridge; Mr. J. Lancashire, Bury New Road, Whitefield; Mr. J. Spencer, 70 Bolton Street, Ramsbottom; and Mr. G. Fairbrother, 13 Benfield Terrace, Heywood. *Deputy Registrars*—Mr. Fred Wild, 35 Walmersley Road, Bury; Mr. Thomas John Tuke, Sunny Villa, Bamford, near Rochdale; Mr. Wm. Hamilton, Unsworth Pole; Mr. Thomas Butterworth, Bolton Road, Hazlehurst, Ramsbottom; and Mr. George A. Fairbrother, 13 Benfield Terrace, Heywood.

Surrogates for granting Licenses for Marriages to be solemnised in churches or chapels of the Established Church within the Bury district, are: *Bury*—Rev. R. Hudson, Rev. W. J. Löwenberg. *Elton*—Rev. E. Westerman. *Radcliffe*—Rev. E. Fletcher. *Ramsbottom*—Rev. W. H. Corbould.

Births and Deaths.

BURY NORTH DISTRICT—*Registrar*—Mr. Joseph Melling, 49 Cateaton Street; office, 43 Parson's Lane; office hours, 10 to 11 a.m., 2-30 to 4 p.m. daily, Monday, 6 to 7. Office closed on Monday and Saturday afternoons. BURY SOUTH—*Registrar*—Mr. S. Holt, 6 School Brow; hours of attendance, Monday and Thursday mornings, 10 to 12, afternoons, 2 to 3, evenings, 6 to 7, other days mornings only, 10 to 11. BIRTLE—*Registrar*—Mr. G. Ashworth, Hooley Bridge, Heywood. ELTON—*Registrar*—Mrs. Annie Smethurst, 23 Park View Terrace, Ainsworth Road, Elton. HEYWOOD—*Registrar*—Mr. G. Fairbrother, 13 Benfield Terrace, Heywood. HOLCOMBE—*Registrar*—Mr. Jas. Spencer, 70 Bolton Street, Ramsbottom. PILKINGTON *Registrar*—Mr. John Lancashire, Assistant Overseer, Clevelands, Whitefield. RADCLIFFE—*Registrar*—Mr. Richard Ellerbeck, 25 Sunny Mount, Spring Lane, Radcliffe. TOTTINGTON-LOWER-END—*Registrar*—Mr. John Farraday, Market Street, Tottington. WALMERSLEY—*Registrar*—Mr. James Nuttall, Assistant Overseer, Shuttleworth.

POLITICAL.

CONSERVATIVE.

Bury Central Conservative Club.

Broad Street. *President*—W. O. Walker, Esq. *Chairman of Committee*—Mr. J. T. Newbold. *Hon. Sec.*—Mr. F. Howarth. *Secretary*—Mr. J. Shaw. *Treasurer*—Mr. G. Yates.

Elton Conservative Hall Co., Limited.

Chairman and Treasurer—Henry Whitehead, Esq. *Secretary*—Captain Pilkington.

Elton Conservative Working Men's Club

President—Mr. Samuel Walker. *Treasurer*—Mr. Wm. Kirkman. *Secretary*—Mr. Charles Openshaw. *Steward*—Joseph Jackson.

The other Conservative Clubs are

The Stanley, Manchester Road; Beaconsfield, Union Square; Salisbury, Moorgate; Roach, Rochdale Road; Churchill, Fernhill; and Limefield and Woolfold.

LIBERAL.

Trevelyan Club.

President—E. G. Wrigley, Esq. *Treasurer*—Mr. Thomas Roberts. *Hon. Secretary*—Mr. Oswald Wild.

Cobden Club (Walmersley Road).

President—R. Crossland, Esq. *Treasurer*—Mr. Thomas Holt. *Secretary*—Mr. H. Lightbown.

Elton Liberal Club.

President—Mr. Cornelius Farrer. *Secretary*—Mr. Alfred Hamer. *Steward*—Joseph Scholes.

The other Liberal Clubs are

The Gladstone, Parsonage Street; Philips', Ormerod Street; Fishpool, Blackford Bridge and Heap Bridge.

Michael Davitt Club (21, Fleet Street, & 14, Market Street).

President—Mr. James Rose. *Treasurer*—Mr. John Kennedy. *Secretary*—Mr. James McKenna.

Registration Agents.

Borough—*Conservative*—Mr. Squire Holt, School Brow. *Liberal*—Mr. Henry Seal. County (Heywood Division)—*Conservative*—Mr. E. Griffiths, Castle Chambers, Bury.

RELIGIOUS.

Church of England.

Parish Church (St. Mary's)*.—Rector, Rev. E. J. G. Hornby, Rectory. Curates; Rev. A. Anderton, Bradford Terrace; Rev. T. G. Cox, 16, Knowsley Street. Notices of Marriages, Baptisms, &c., should be given to Mr. Samuel Bailey, Clerk, Union Square. **Marriages may be solemnised at the Parish Church where one or both parties reside in the district of St. Thomas' or Peter's.

**St. John's Church, Stanley-St.*—Vicar, Rev. R. Hudson, M.A., Walmersley Road. Curate, Rev. Jenkyn Griffiths, 27, Parsons Lane.
**St. Mark's Church.*—Vicar, Rev. J. M. Maddox, M.A., 14, Malvern Villas, Chesham.
**St. Paul's Church.*—Vicar, Rev. J. Chell, Vicarage, Parsonage Street.
**St. Peter's Church, Redvales.*—Rev. W. J. Löwenberg, Starkies.
**St. Stephens' Church, Elton.*—Vicar, Rev. R. P. Linfield, 55, Belbeck Street.
**St. Thomas' Church, Rochdale Road.*—Vicar, Rev. J. Williams, Wilson Street. Curate, Rev. E. G. Baker, B.A.
**Trinity Church, Spring Street.*—Vicar, Rev. J. C. Hordern; Curate, Rev. W. Trusted, 24, Heywood Street.
**All Saints' Church, Elton.*—Vicar, Rev. E. Westerman (Surrogate), Vicarage, Tottington road; Curates, Revs. J. Durnford, Park view, Walshaw road, and J. Proude, B.A., 129 Vicarage view, Tottington road.

Dissenters.

**Baptist Chapel (Ebenezer), Knowsley Street.*—Rev. Benjamin Bowker, 149, Bell Lane.
**Baptist Chapel (Providence), Freetown.*—Rev. R. Moxon, 75, Bridge Street.
**Baptist Chapel, Chesham.*—Rev. John Harper, St. Anne's Street, Chesham.
**Congregational Chapel, New Road.*—Rev. J. Macrae Simcock, Limefield.
**Congregational Chapel (Bethel), Henry Street.*—Rev. Chas. Ashford, B.A., 84, Milton Terrace.
**Congregational Chapel, Castle Croft.*—Rev. H. A. Lawson, M.A., Woodfield House.
**Congregational Church, Blackford Bridge.*—Rev. W. Nichols.
**Christian Church, Rochdale Road.*—Vacant.
Free Gospel School, Kay Street.—Supplies.
**Methodist New Connexion Church, Heywood Street.*—Rev. E. Holyoake, 5, Heywood Street.
New Jerusalem Church, Walmersley Road.
**Primitive Methodist Chapel, Walmersley Road.*—Rev. E. Alford, 13, Canning Street, Walmersley Road.——*Elton.*—Supplies.——*Croft Street.*
United Methodist Free Church (Brunswick), North Street.*—Rev. T. W. Townsend, Woodfields House, Fernhill; and Rev. John Taylor, 255, Rochdale Road.——Heap Bridge (Bethel Chapel).*——*Limefield.*——*Elton.*—A. J. Mahomet, lay minister.—*Park Hills.*—Rev. John Mather.——*Higher Woodhill.*
**Welsh Presbyterian Chapel, Benson Street.*—Rev. Edward Humphreys.
**Wesleyan Chapels, Union Street*—Rev. R. Harding, 10, Tenterden Street; Rev. W. J. Boote, 14, St. Mary's Place; Rev. J. Rhodes, Summerseat.—*Pits o'th' Moor—Russell Street—Elton—Woolfold—Walshaw Lane.*

Roman Catholic Churches.

**St. Marie's*, Manchester Road—The Rev. M. Byrne (M.R.)
**St. Joseph's*, Peter Street—Rev. J. Fraser, Peter Street; Assistant: the Rev. P. Graham.
Our Lady of Good Counsel and Guardian Angels (School-Chapel), Walshaw Road, Elton—Rev. B. C. Pozzi, 104, Tottington Road.

Those Marked thus (*) are Licensed for Marriages.

Bury Young Men's Christian Association.

16, and 18, Haymarket Street. Established March 31st, 1875. *Treasurer*—Mr. John Driffield, Seedfield. *Treasurer*—Mr. James Wilkinson. *Gen. Sec.*—Mr. W. G. Wood. *Gymnastic Instructor*—Mr. Arthur Burrows.

TRADES AND FRIENDLY.

Trades' Club Houses in Bury.

Amalgamated Iron Trades, Queen's Hotel. *Amalgamated Iron Trades*, (No. 2 branch) Roebuck Inn. *Amalgamated Railway Servants*, Royal Hotel, Silver Street. *Amalgamated Carpenters and Joiners*, Knowsley Hotel. *Boiler Makers*, Church Inn, Spring Street. *Brass Finishers*, Hand and Shears. *Bricklayers*, King's Head, King Street. *Brickmakers*, Bay Horse. *Bury and Elton Cardroom Association*, 16, Market Street. *Butchers*, Knowsley Hotel. *Cloggers*, Commercial Inn. *Cabinetmakers*, Knowsley Hotel. *Coachmakers*, Royal Hotel. *Engineers*, Coach and Horses, Princess Street. *Hatters*, Clarence Hotel. *Mill Managers and Overlookers*, Queen's Hotel. *Metal Planers, Shapers, and Slotters*, Cricketers' Inn, Mosses. *Machine Printers*, Hand and Shears. *Machine, Engine, and Iron Grinders' Society*, Clay Bank Hotel. *Moulders*, Rochdale Road. *Moulders* (No. 1), Queen Inn, Badgers Street. *Plumbers and Glaziers*, White Lion. *Painters*, Boar's Head, Water Street. *Pattern Makers*, White Lion, Bolton Street. *Power-Loom Overlookers* (No. 10 Branch), Clarence Hotel. *Saddlers*, Stanley Arms, Stanley Street. *Shoemakers*, Globe Inn, The Wylde. *Spindle and Fly Makers*, Knowsley Hotel. *Spinners*, Hand and Shears. *Steam Engine Makers* (No. 1 branch), Clarence Hotel. *Steam Engine Makers* (No. 2 branch), Swan Inn. *Stonemasons*, White Bear. *Tailors*, Alma Hotel, King Street. *Tinplate Workers*, Queen's Hotel. *Tape Sizers*, Knowsley Hotel. *Wheelwrights and Blacksmiths*, Hand and Shears, Fleet Street. *Bury and Elton District Weavers' Association*, 16, Market Street.

Co-operative Provision Society.

President—Mr. Owen Thomas. *Treasurer*—Mr. Henry Scholes. *Secretary*—Mr. T. Killon. *Cashier*—Mr. E. Lonsdale. *Manager*—Mr. W. Wild. *Sub-Manager*—Mr. Jas. Holden. *Librarian*—Mrs. Peers. *Assistant Librarian*—Miss Olive. The Library contains about 13,000 volumes, and is open daily, except on Sunday and Tuesday afternoons, during the following hours, viz.:—Morning from 9-30 to 12 o'clock; Afternoon, from 1-30 to to 4-30; Evening, from 6 to 9. News Room open daily—8 a.m. to 10 p.m. Sundays—1 to 8 p.m.

Brunswick Temperance Society.

President—Rev. T. W. Townend. *Secretaries*—Messrs. H. Fletcher and Thos. Kay. *Registrars*—Messrs. J. Smith, T. Ormerod, M. Hargreaves, and the Secretaries. *Choir Master*—Mr. J. W. Gaunt. *Assistant*—Mrs. Barnes. Committee of 70 persons.

Beersellers' Association.

Chairman—Mr. J. Counsell, Hornby Street. *Vice-Chairman*—Mr. T. Fletcher. *Treasurer*—Mr. Wm. Robinson. *Secretary*—Mr. John Heyes, Union Street. Meet on Wednesday every four weeks, at members' houses in rotation.

Juvenile Foresters' Society.

Treasurer—Mr. E. Ditchfield, 7 Walmersley Road. *Secretary*—Mr. J. H. Shaw, 4 Cooper Street. *Collectors*—Messrs. J. Driver, W. Wilkes, and J. Livsey. Quarterly Meetings held on Jan. 12th, April 12th, July 12th, and Oct. 11th.

Licensed Victuallers' Association.

Chairman—Mr. Joseph Metcalf. *Vice-Chairman*—Mr. J. C. Ainsworth. *Treasurer*—Mr. Joseph Frost. *Secretary*—Mr. Edmund Whittam, 202 Bolton Street. The Meetings are held on the last Thursday in each month.